YOKING SCIE
AND RELIGI

Ralph Wendell Burhoe in 1980.

YOKING SCIENCE AND RELIGION
The Life and Thought of
Ralph Wendell Burhoe

by David R. Breed

FOREWORD BY
Roger W. Sperry

ZYGON BOOKS
CHICAGO

Copyright © 1992 by
the Joint Publication Board of *Zygon*

Cover art by
Corrine Niedenthal
Chicago, Illinois

Library of Congress Catalog Number: 91-67648
ISBN 0-9618233-1-3

Published by Zygon Books.
Zygon: Journal of Religion and Science
The Chicago Center for Religion and Science
1100 E. 55th St.
Chicago, IL 60615

Contents

Foreword

by Roger W. Sperry

To join mainline religion and science, even to bring the two into ami-
cable dialogue on their respective aims and differences, is something
to which many eminent persons and groups have aspired. In the long
history of such efforts, however, none appears to have achieved more
wide and lasting positive impact than the venture described here by
David R. Breed in his account of the thought and life work of Ralph
Wendell Burhoe. That venture has included the founding of the Institute on Religion in an Age of Science (IRAS) and the associated *Zygon:
Journal of Religion and Science*. Almost from the start, both have received
international recognition and respect both in theology and in science,
and continue today to furnish a leading ongoing forum for these two
great competing systems of belief with their different approaches and
different answers to humanity's deepest questions.

The achievements of Ralph Burhoe are all the more remarkable
when we remember that religion and science are often categorized as
archenemies or the antithesis of one another. They traditionally proceed from different starting assumptions with different frames of
reasoning and are widely appraised as "mutually exclusive realms of
human thought." In addition, the two disciplines often propound
notoriously divergent views on issues in some of society's most sensitive
and crucial areas, including that of the sacred. All in all, the sustained
success record of IRAS and *Zygon* in bringing religion and science
together in constructive discourse is high tribute to the guiding
perspectives of their founder and leader.

It is of interest to ask accordingly, What special features in these
projects have been responsible for their success where other efforts
with quite similar aims have had much less impact? A full in-depth
answer would undoubtedly concern a sizable complex of factors with
collective interactions. However, I plan in what follows to focus on just
two features in Burhoe's guidance that seem to me to have been particularly important that help to set off Burhoe's approach from various
other efforts to join religion and science.

The first feature I have in mind is the stated guiding policy within
IRAS and *Zygon* that the effort to join science and religion must be

firmly based on solid mainstream science, not on esoteric fringe activities or minority opinions or theories that might try to pass as science. Burhoe relied on scientific views near what he called "the top center of recent scientific development." In other words, concepts and developments such as Gaia theory, the anthropic principle, morphic fields, the Tao of physics, panpsychism, paranormal phenomena, and other quasi-scientific concepts and views that as yet lack genuine mainstream acceptance must neither be relied upon nor allowed to alter (especially not to dominate) the image, policies, or practice of the effort.

To resist the attractions of such fringe developments, however, is often not easy in the face of ever-present pressures to find more comforting answers than those traditionally advanced by basic science. Over some three centuries fundamental science has depicted a strictly physically driven, mindless, and deterministic cosmos devoid of purpose, value, caring, or higher meaning, a world-picture that reduces the human psyche, and indeed the whole of our existence, to ultimate meaninglessness.

Any possible oversight or chink in the foundations of this stark picture tends naturally to receive eager welcome. A group or institute trying to join science and religion, but also wishing to grow and acquire increased support, is bound to find that potential members and donors are much more attracted when the rigorous mainstream standards are relaxed. Once such a trend gets started, however, it tends to snowball through subsequent decisions and planning to swing ever further from basic science. The predictable result is to degrade the project's credibility and the main significance of the whole effort to join science and religion.

The essence and strength of science demands rigorous adherence to time-tested principles. The policy in IRAS and *Zygon* to stand firm in this regard would seem to have contributed in no small part to their continuing sound standing and high professional regard.

What about such a policy, however, during the occasional rare period of revolutionary transition when mainstream science is undergoing a shift in its foundational concepts—for example, as in the time of Copernicus or Darwin? In such a transition period, how long does one hold to the old established paradigm before accepting the new? At what point does a growing radical fringe development qualify as fundamental mainstream science?

The question becomes of increasing concern today in view of mounting indications that science currently is undergoing just such a genuine shift in its basic paradigm for causal explanation. Traditional reductive physicalism, with its atomistic, microdeterministic interpretations of both human and nonhuman nature, is increasingly being challenged and displaced in many areas of science by a new antireductive, wholistic, and mentalistic epistemology.

The emerging new antireductive paradigm had its start in a revolt in behavioral science, a revolt that turned around the previous acausal status of mind and consciousness (the so-called cognitive, mentalist, or consciousness revolution of the early 1970s). This conceptual turnabout, putting conscious, subjective qualities in a new causal role, was achieved, however, only by invoking a different concept of causal determinism—in effect, by changing the rules and framework for causal explanation.

Instead of assuming physical reality to be fully understood and completely determined through its parts from below upward, the new outlook claims that things are also causally determined from above downward by emergent supervenient properties that are irreducible. This "double-way" principle of causality has wide application throughout nature at all levels and, accordingly, has since been gaining acceptance in many other areas. In other words, what started as an intradisciplinary revolt seems now to be turning into a major paradigm shift throughout science.

Already this shift has reached a stage where one finds it difficult to judge whether the new model or the old reductive physicalism ought to be accepted as the dominant explanatory paradigm of mainstream science. Among the more visible advances to date, the new paradigm has alrady served for some two decades as the reigning foundational doctrine in behavioral science. It has come into extensive use also in the related human and social sciences, has transformed general systems theory and become its dominant feature, has attained dominance also in the field of animal awareness, and has made strong impacts in evolutionary theory and epistemology. It has led to a "new science of life," a new "hierarchy theory," and what has been called a new "science of qualities." More recently, it has begun to be adopted also within neuroscience and to penetrate via chaos and computer science even into physics, the recognized stronghold of reductive physicalism. Many of these foregoing developments with their implications are today being welcomed in a so-called postmodern movement in theology.

The double-way or macro-mental view of causality upholds a vastly revised scientific cosmology that is enormously more amenable than that of traditional physicalism to the yoking of science and religion. A subjectivist and wholistic epistemology turns around the long-accepted science-value dichotomy and suggests a new answer for the age-old paradox of free will and determinism, an answer that blends both determinism and free will in a new framework and preserves moral responsibility.

In view of such changes, can science today still be said to depict an atomistic, quantum mechanics universe? Or, has science moved to a new world picture in which emergent mental and other macro properties are causal, irreducible, and ineliminable, a new paradigm that logically legitimates the derivation of ultimate value from the worldview of science? What position has Burhoe maintained during this transitional period; and what has been the effect on policy in IRAS and *Zygon*?

Burhoe himself was close to this paradigm shift at its start. He was present at its first public expression in a lecture series entitled "New Views of the Nature of Man," presented in the spring of 1965 at the University of Chicago and organized by the futurist-physicist John Platt. This is where I first met Ralph Burhoe, introduced by a mutual friend, Dwight Ingle, during refreshments in a quiet spot after the lecture.

Burhoe himself at about this time published his own suggestions concerning a wholistic epistemology, elaborated in a fashion that acknowledges the "double-way" principle of causality. He focused on a hierarchic view of values in which life, or "viability" is the primary, highest, or ultimate value. Burhoe conceived the hierarchic value system to be evolved in five successively higher, more complex, stages via natural selection in a self-organizing "negentropic" process of emergent evolution. Starting with the genotypic, the determinants rise through cerebral, cultural, rational, and finally, at the top, the scientific, which he placed above theological rationalizing. The higher, more evolved values must conform with their genotypic foundation but at the same time may supersede and control the lower-level determinants. Burhoe did not himself raise the involved reductionist-wholistic issues which at that time were still in a period of relative neglect but, within a few years, would explode into a new prominence that continues today.

Judging from Burhoe's comments at the 1965 lecture series and also from his subsequent writings, one may infer the presence of another feature in his guidance that also helped to steer a carefully mixed middle course amenable both to religion and to science. The strategy in this case consists in taking care to stay clear of embroilments in the underlying philosophical issues where science and religion pointedly differ and where oftentimes the antagonisms are most intense and the viewpoints most incompatible.

Rather than probe the pros and cons of such philosophic underpinnings, Burhoe has preferred to take science and its tenets at the going face value, meanwhile applying himself to relatively neutral issues such as an improved scientific explanation of altrusim. Whether conscious and intentional or more an intuitional sense of how best to achieve his aim, this strategically wise detachment was manifest also on another occasion in reference to the then-prevailing philosophic bans against the derivation of ethical or moral values from the facts of science.

The long-accepted fact-value dichotomy now becomes logically reversed in the new mentalist paradigm which integrates science and values in a whole new scientific interpretation of the status, role, and objective power of subjective values in determining the course of human affairs. The revised new outlook can be seen to have particular relevance in the context of our mounting global crises and threats to survival.

I tried to spell all this out more explicitly for the first time in a manuscript submitted early in 1972 to editor Dwight Ingle in Chicago, where Ralph Burhoe, his friend and colleague, would presumably be a principal (and predictably sympathetic) referee. Though Burhoe's career-long efforts to merge science and religious values gained strong reinforcement and new heightened urgency in these arguments and took on a new vigor, Burhoe himself consistently avoided tying his envisioned goal to any new philosophic polemic.

Again, this seems to have been the wiser course in the light of subsequent developments. Immediate reactions to the proposed new outlook by both ethicists and scientists consisted predominantly of heated rejection. Only slowly over the years have the rejections gradually became dissolved; now they have turned around in what is recognized as a new era in respect to the treatment of values.

Looking back, we see that Burhoe's effort to join science and religious values was launched during a period when the leading philosophic doctrine of the day, not only within professional philosophy but widely shared also in science and among the thinking public at large, proclaimed that what Burhoe was proposing to do could not be done: Values, we were taught, "cannot be derived from the facts of science." "Science can tell us *how* but not *why.*" "The *naturalistic fallacy* is inescapable." "Values lie beyond the realm of science." "Scientific determinism abolishes free will, choice, and thus any moral responsibility"—and so on. Such deterrents and the related back-up thinking of the kind that prevailed in the 1950s and '60s agreed in predicting that a task of the kind Burhoe envisioned was not merely unconventional and difficult; it was logically impossible.

Today, prevailing opinion on these same issues, swayed by the new emergent and subjectivist principles of two-way causal explanation, has undergone a diametric turnaround. In some ways the consciousness revolution might equally well be called a values revolution. In any case, our currently prevailing mainstream opinion tells us that Ralph Wendell Burhoe's aim, holding firm against shifting winds in philosophy and pragmatically centered in science as it is practiced, has been from the start in the right direction.

Preface

This book is a result of work done in the course of my doctoral program in theology and science. The roots of the book are deep, stretching back to my childhood at a time when my intellectual capacities were developing. Since that time I have been intensely interested in the religious depths of life and the physical world in which I participate. The sciences, most particularly physics, have always held a compelling fascination for me. The sciences challenged me to comprehend those fundamental processes through which understanding of the behavior of things is possible. My religious training and spiritual discipline challenged me to see all things as related to God the creator. These interests set the course of my intellectual pilgrimage. For me, the quest for a scientific understanding of the fundamental processes of the physical world and the quest for a theological understanding of how all things are related to God have always been the same quest. In my naivete, I took it for granted that others perceived the quest for understanding in the same way.

In my college years I discovered that what I took for granted was not widely shared. Instead, I increasingly found others for whom religion and science were two distinct pathways. For many, the religious and the scientific dimensions of human life were not compatible, let alone aspects of the same journey of understanding. Through my study, I discovered a long history of thinkers writing about problems concerning the tension between a scientific, rational conceptuality and a religious, spiritual appreciation of the world. With the burgeoning of the sciences and technology in the past century, the tension has become magnified and with it the numbers of thinkers and writers engaging its problems.

It is not enough to have a naive intuition about the unified character of life. Such an intuition needs to be expressed in language in order for one to become aware of its shape and character, to communicate it to another, and to assess and debate its cogency and veracity. During my seminary studies I wrote an essay on a theology of chaos which brought together evolutionary theory, thermodynamics, Christian theology, and the integrative thought of Teilhard de Chardin. It was in the preparation of that essay that I first met Ralph Burhoe. I found his articles and those of other authors in *Zygon* to be excellent resources. His ideas, reflections, and questions were helpful. I later became active in the Institute on Religion in an Age of Science (IRAS) and participated in the seminars on religion and science that met in Ralph's living room. Here was another person struggling to articulate his own vision of an integrated perspective on religion and science. In him I found the unified, but two-fold, concern for the religious and the scientific depths of human experience. Although the participants in the seminars did not always agree, we all appreciated the stimulation and intellectual challenge of wrestling with his formulations. I was especially attracted by his graciousness, openness, and his intense desire to formulate theoretical interpretations of religious phenomena and doctrines in the light of scientific understanding that were debatable on scientific as well as religious and theological grounds.

When the time for selection of a subject for my dissertation project approached, the possibility of a study of the thought of Ralph Burhoe was met with a cautious, albeit encouraging, response from my advisor, Philip Hefner. As I began my study, reading, and interviewing, I found that I needed to construct a written account of Burhoe's life and thought, because such a resource was not available. This phase of the project expanded and eventually formed the main body of the dissertation itself. In the process I learned that in order to understand a person's thought, one must understand how it developed in the context of the particular circumstances of that person's life. This book, then, is a product of my examination of the factors and circumstances of life in which Ralph Burhoe's thought developed.

Ralph Burhoe made available papers and records from his personal files. Without his generosity this study could not have been accomplished, for the necessary materials would not have been accessible. He contributed greatly to this project with his encouragement, sharing his memories and carefully reading many drafts. He and his wife, Calla, generously shared their hospitality on my innumerable visits to their home. Calla, who has energetically supported Ralph's work, also contributed to this project with generous encouragement and careful reading of the drafts for accuracy and intelligibility of communication. In so many ways, this book was written for them, and it is to them that it is dedicated.

In the course of the writing of this book, I received support and encouragement from many other people as well. First was the untiring love and endurance of my wife, Ann. Without her support this work would simply not have been possible. My children, Michael and Hannah, gave great joy and showed remarkable patience. Philip Hefner gave guidance and support throughout the project and encouraged its publication. Karl Peters helped give a needed perspective at many points along the way. Carol Gorski has worked the magic of the editor to craft a book from a cauldron of prose aimed at a different purpose. I owe a debt of gratitude to the Lutheran School of Theology at Chicago, the Jesuit-Kraus-McCormick Library, and Meadville/ Lombard Theological School for the resources they provided to produce this study.

Finally I wish to acknowledge a number of colleagues who have contributed to this project in many various ways: Carl Braaten, Don Browning, Richard Busse, Robert Butterfield, Ronald Engel, John Godbey, Lynn Hubbard, Roy Morrison, Arthur Peacocke, David Priestley, George Riggan, Jay Rochelle, Michael Ruse, Robert Russell, Widick Schroeder, Malcolm Sutherland, and Vitor Westhelle. Many people associated with the Institute on Religion in an Age of Science have listened and added to my thinking in the course of writing this study. I also wish to acknowledge with thanks all of my family, friends, colleagues, and teachers who over the years of my life have contributed in many different ways to the outcome of this project.

—David R. Breed

I Perceiving the Problem and Envisioning Its Solution, 1911-1954

Ralph Wendell Burhoe was born 21 June 1911, in Somerville, Massachusetts, into a seriously pious family. Many years later, reminiscing upon his early years, he wrote:

In my childhood I had readily believed my parents' religious tradition, but already in high school science I began to experience how religious belief tended to be eroded whenever the religious teachings became doubtful in the context of seemingly more reliable truth. Since my Baptist tradition purported to persuade on the basis of reasonable evidence of truth, I was early involved in various attempts to resolve the puzzle of what is truth (Burhoe 1981, 14).

Nevertheless, these puzzles and incongruities of life not only continued but intensified:

I experienced dreams tinged with religious awe and fear concerning my destiny. And struggling with either long spells of sickness or maladaptive social situations, rational and behavioral incongruities taxed my emotional equilibrium, leading to states of despair which were from time to time transcended by joyous mystical insights which gave me new courage and new attitudes and behavior patterns to overcome the otherwise seemingly unbearable conditions. I was at once severely rational and mystical (Burhoe 1964a, 3).

These reminiscences point to the emergence of one central concern for Burhoe: to preserve the credibility of traditional religious wisdom and personal religious experience in the face of a scientific world that threatened to dissolve religious belief with a more reliable truth.

PHILOSOPHY AND THE SCIENCES AT HARVARD

Entering Harvard in 1928 at age seventeen, Burhoe began an intellectually formative period. A survey course in Western philosophy, given by Ralph Barton Perry, made a lasting impression, along with such members of the faculty as W. E. Hocking and Alfred North

Whitehead. William James's shadow loomed large in the lecture hall, and the Socratic dialogues and Spinoza impressed him with the power of reason to make sense out of essentially religious problems. But he thought that more recent philosophy was wanting in both its capacity to deal with religious problems and to reveal reality vis-à-vis the sciences.

Burhoe "became convinced that the sciences were our most advanced tools for discovering what was true and [he] studied them widely" (Burhoe 1981, 14). He studied physics with Frederick A. Saunders and Edwin C. Kemble, biology with G. H. Parker, and physical anthropology with E. A. Hooten. Hooten's course was Burhoe's first extensive introduction to theories of human evolution. For explaining why humans evolved, Hooten favored a "triumphant intelligence theory" that emphasized the importance of the brain in evolution. As the following passage shows, Hooten espoused a form of the argument from design.

One cannot conclude a volume of facts, reflections, and speculations concerning the course of human evolution without asking himself if there is any place for a guiding intelligence in this marvelous progression of organic events. That evolution has occurred I have not the slightest doubt. That it is an accidental or chance occurrence I do not believe, although chance probably has often intervened and is an important contributing factor. But if evolution is not mainly a chance process it must be an intelligent or purposeful process. It seems to me quite immaterial whether we believe that the postulated source of intelligence or purposeful causation is a divine being or set of natural "laws." What difference does it make whether God is Nature or Nature is God? The pursuit of natural causes either leads to the deification of nature, or to the recognition of the supernatural, or to a simple admission of ignorance, bewilderment, and awe. It should arouse the feeling of reverence in any one who attempts to grasp the central phenomenon which emerges from the vast assemblage of organic facts. . . . Whether man arose from the apes or was made from mud, he is in a sense a divine product. Organic evolution is an achievement not unworthy of any God and not incompatible with the loftiest conception of religion. . . . Theories of origin and causation are often transient and evanescent; life itself can never fail to command the interest and evoke the inquiry of human minds (Hooten 1931, 604–5).

The kind of ideas exemplified in this passage bear a striking similarity to ideas that Burhoe later developed: the importance of the brain in human evolution; the equivalence of God and nature; affirmation that the source of evolution is God, conceived in terms of the natural selection of living organisms according to the laws of nature; and the centrality of life.

Following a suggestion that the psychological sciences might be of more interest for religious or value problems than philosophy and the natural sciences, in his sophomore and junior years Burhoe shifted his attention from the physical to the psychological sciences. He studied general psychology under E. G. Boring (of the Titchener School), experimental psychology under J. G. Beebe-Center, and a social psychology course taught by Gordon Allport.

Part of the reading for the latter course was W. B. Cannon's newly published *Wisdom of the Body*, and Cannon also chose the title of the 1923 Harvey Oration of E. H. Sterling, to express conviction in the great value of the experimental method for the solution of biological problems. According to Cannon, "Only by understanding the wisdom of the body . . . shall we attain that 'mastery of disease and pain which will enable us to relieve the burden of mankind' " (Cannon 1932, xv). He also coined the term *homeostasis* to designate the coordinated physiological processes that, in highly evolved animals, maintain a fairly stable internal environment through self-righting adjustments that minimize the effects of changes in the external environment and potentially lethal conditions induced by stress. Developing the concept of homeostasis, Cannon presented research on the relation of the autonomic nervous system to the self-regulation of physiological processes. The concept of homeostasis firmly rooted itself in Burhoe's thought. Throughout his later writings it served as a key integrating notion for understanding the nature of living systems.

During the Harvard years, Burhoe's guiding concern was not social respectability or vocational preparation; rather, it was a quest to construct a solid foundation for meaning and direction in life, "since the supports undergirding the sacred meaning of my life had crumbled under me by their rational and ontological insufficiency." Burhoe viewed himself as a vagabond and prier into the realms of learning, an intellectual maverick. Of his third year at Harvard he remarked,

I vagabonded, as the Harvard Crimson then called it, almost as many courses as I took officially, ranging from Alfred North Whitehead, with his high-pitched voice which I did not very well appreciate then, to a course that visited industrial-chemical plants. . . . But as fascinating as the university was in opening doors on new systems of rationality and empirically validated understanding, I was disenchanted because I did not find a clear vision that the intellectual apparatus would add up to anything significant for life. I was not at all concerned with social respectability or a vocation to earn a living (Burhoe 1964a, 4, 7).

Together with the fact that an economic depression wiped out his father's modest fortune and health, and having been persuaded against steaming to Europe as a stowaway to sample the educational situation in a French university and communistic philosophy,

Burhoe left Harvard to explore "the nature of people and society in various parts of New England, ostensibly as a salesman of different kinds in different places" (Burhoe 1964a, 7).

BAPTIST CAMPUS MINISTRY

During his college years Burhoe had been involved in a Baptist campus ministry group under Newton C. Fetter, who was commissioned by the denomination to work full-time with students in the Boston area. As Burhoe saw it, Fetter was like his father: a moderate, semiliberal Baptist, with strict, old-fashioned moral conviction, who was open to modern knowledge. (One aspect of the ministry was a Sunday evening program, where Burhoe met his first wife.) One of the speakers at Sunday evening meetings, Kirtley F. Mather, impressed Burhoe with his apparent combination of good science and genuine religious concern. A renowned geologist, Mather had recently testified for evolution at the Scopes "Monkey" Trial. (Almost two decades later Burhoe became the first executive officer of the American Academy of Arts and Sciences, a newly created position resulting from the findings of the Commission on the Present Status and Future of the Academy, chaired by Mather.)

Burhoe attributed his passion for religious problems to emotional sensitivity and empathy with the suffering he saw around him, which aroused the desire to understand its sources. From early childhood, he said, he had been impressed by the widespread discontents, confusions, and sufferings of acquaintances. Reflecting on his attempts to understand the factors underlying emotional discontent and disturbances, he wrote:

I was sometimes a bum among bums in a flophouse, sometimes a bum riding in a car with a stranger where self revelations can outstrip the psychiatrist's couch, sometimes a house-to-house salesman of silk stockings, encyclopedias, or insurance talking alone with a frustrated or injured soul, where I found myself far more interested in understanding the person's problems than with making a sale to earn my way through college. . . . I saw the sources of divorce, murder, theft, and all manner of personal and social injustice; of bitterness, alcoholism, and insanity. These forms of derangement and suffering seemed to me far vaster and more important than the First World War, which had not affected me very much directly; moreover, I saw in these kinds of states in the minds of men the very sources of the collective disruptions of war. This extended survey of the intimate feelings, attitudes, and thinking of a broad sample of human beings . . . was perhaps my most persistent area of study and the richest source of understanding. I have never found from reading the second-hand artistic portrayals of all this such a sense of truth of the human predicament (Burhoe 1964a, 6).

His empathy with suffering humanity and the desire to understand its underlying factors were important for Burhoe, for it is on behalf of this human predicament that a sound and effective religion must offer hope for salvation. Burhoe's interpretation of religion was developed as an answer to what he later came to see as the fundamental problem underlying human suffering: loss of credibility and confidence in religion has deprived many humans of attitudes and beliefs that are essential for moral guidance, meaning, motivation, and a healthy and fulfilling life.

"On a honeymoon hike over the Presidential Range of the White Mountains we [Burhoe and wife] decided I should go back to college and perhaps prepare for the ministry" (Burhoe 1964a, 8). With Frances's support, he took more courses in psychology and anthropology at Harvard, but financial conditions made it seem impossible to make up the "lost" courses he needed for the degree.

ANDOVER-NEWTON THEOLOGICAL SCHOOL

Burhoe's great-uncle had been a Baptist preacher, and Burhoe's father had hoped that his son might follow in the uncle's footsteps; so he encouraged his son to consider the ministry. In the summer of 1932 Burhoe's father arranged a luncheon with Harry Emerson Fosdick, who happened to be in Boston, to persuade Burhoe to go to theological school. His father found financial support, and young Burhoe was able to bypass requirements for a bachelor's degree and enter Andover-Newton Theological School in the fall. He recalled: "My burning question was 'What ails religion and how do you make something out of it in this intellectual climate?' " (Burhoe 1985, conversation with Breed). Evidently, he was not able to find sufficient support to sustain his interest, for he later wrote: "In spite of some good men on the faculty, I found the school . . . out of touch with what I thought were the realities of the intellect and the world." Because the economic depression continued and his wife lost her job, he quit school in November to look for work but found nothing. After they sold his car (for $50), they "withdrew from civilization to meditate upon [their situation], hibernating in a log cabin on the side of Mount Washington." Returning to Boston in the spring, they lived on a boat tied up between the slums of the North End and the Navy Yard (Burhoe 1964a, 8).

They attended Community Church (under Clarence Skinner) and later First Church (under Charles Edward Park), and at First Church Burhoe worked with a youth group, which persuaded him to give theological education another try. He returned to Andover-Newton in February 1935 "to explore my prime concern: to find a way to interpret religion credibly in the light of the sciences'' (Burhoe 1964a, 14). Among his teachers were Amos Wilder, in New Testament, and Richard Cabot, head of medicine at Massachusetts General Hospital, who had been his adviser when Burhoe was a freshman at Harvard. Reflecting on this second—and last—attempt, Burhoe wrote:

I was basically sympathetic with the general aims and functions of religion, and my attitude was to explore more tolerantly or patiently what wisdom and practices might be there. There was good liberal scholarship on the Bible, and pioneering work on relationships with psychiatry and the social sciences with laboratory visits to various kinds of institutions. Dwight Bradley impressed me as a liberal intellect who believed the social ethics he taught. Although his theology led him to dub me a genius Anti-Christ, he loved me and I worked with him in his rich suburban Congregational church and later in a church in the growing slums of Boston's South End which was dying as it was trying to integrate racial groups. I had started exploring relations of this religion to the sciences, on my own, but could get no response of significance from faculty or students. Neo-orthodoxy was dawning. My own unorthodoxy did not encourage financial support from the school, and after experience as a summertime pastor in a Universalist-Congregational Church in New Hampshire, in the fall of 1936 my family of two children forced me to quit studies and go to work (Burhoe 1964a, 9–10).

Again for financial but also for other reasons, including dissatisfaction with himself and with traditional religious forms that were not clearly related to scientific understanding, Burhoe was thwarted in his desire to become a religious professional. However, he was more disturbed with his inadequacies, discovered in his theological education and practice in pastoral ministry, than with the function of the religious ministry. Among his limitations he listed his health and his responsibility for supporting his pregnant wife and year-old son—but more important for him was his incapacity to communicate clearly and credibly to his teachers, fellow students, and congregations, and to be taken seriously by them when he tried to confirm religious truth by its proper translation into scientific concepts. His diary for 1935–36 shows that his major goal in returning to theological school had been to make clear the relevance and authenticity of religion in the context of the sciences. He felt that religious truth needed to be confirmed by the sciences and that this confirmation was essential to turn around what seemed to be the decay or impotence of religious faith in an increasingly scientific and technologically dominated culture. If that trend was not reversed, it would result in a sharp decline of moral behavior (Burhoe 1987, memo to Breed).

Among Burhoe's experiences during studies at Andover-Newton (from January 1935 to October 1936), his participation in the Oxford

Group movement (which some called the Buchmanite movement) confirmed his belief that religion needed to be made credible to avoid a decline in moral behavior. The spiritual force of this movement was Frank Buchman, a pietistic Lutheran pastor who had served as visiting lecturer in personal evangelism for the Hartford Seminary Foundation. After a conversion experience Buchman heeded a calling to regenerate the moral fabric of society by concentrating on college campuses.[1] The movement, which eschewed theology, reaffirmed a fundamentalistic evangelical biblical faith upon which it based a restatement of an individualistic moral code in a vocabulary that was thought to be modern, attractive, and effective (see Eister 1950, 209; Clark 1951). The strategy was to get persons, commonly through small-group meetings called house parties, to surrender their will to God-control so that they could listen for divine guidance and perform God's will. Great emphasis was placed on personal piety as governed by the four moral absolutes: honesty, purity, unselfishness, and love.

Burhoe said that he found the house parties impressive and valuable—those autonomous small-group meetings in which individuals confessed their weaknesses, then helped one another correct those weaknesses and more effectively bring about the will of God to regulate their lives as well as their society. He also said that he often felt the Oxford Group's basic weakness was its lack of persuasive objectivity about the will of God and why it is binding. He believed that if the movement could develop credibility about the objectivity of God's will in terms of traditional theology and the modern sciences, it could have become a reformation movement that would have swept the world toward greater peace and justice and thereby transformed it (Burhoe 1987a, 1987b).

Neither the Oxford Group, nor theological school, nor denominational leaders seemed receptive to Burhoe's view that religion could be made more objective and credible for an age of science by translation into the conceptual scheme of modern science. Indeed, it seemed doubtful that any traditional religious group was ready to hear or support him in what he felt needed to be done. This time, therefore, he abandoned his theological education and religious concerns for a scientific occupation, whose demands gave him little time to contemplate religious problems and the human condition.

BLUE HILL YEARS: BURHOE'S SCIENTIFIC PERIOD, 1936–46

Burhoe found employment at the Blue Hill Meteorological Observatory of Harvard University, where he had studied meteorology and climatology as an undergraduate. (He was fondly referred to as "general factotum" by the director, Charles F. Brooks.) After serving as secretary to Brooks, because he was the only one who could type and take shorthand, Burhoe became assistant to the director, helping to manage the staff and ameliorating misunderstandings among one of the most friendly groups with which, he said, he had ever worked. His other duties included librarian, meteorological observation (including occasional night work), and assisting in developing new instrumentation and programs of data collection. One-third of his time was spent in assisting the staff of the American Meteorological Society (Brooks 1937, 14). Although involved mainly with administrative matters, he made a few minor technical contributions, one of which was a technique for measuring average snowfall (Burhoe 1945, 341–42).

The Blue Hill Meteorological Observatory was conceived and constructed by Abbott Lawrence Rotch. "At midnight on 31 January 1885, fireworks were set off, and Rotch commenced a weather observation program that has continued uninterrupted" (see Conover 1985, 30–37). Rotch, who was world-renowned, embarked on a systematic acquisition of meteorological books, research papers, and data, and by the time of his death in 1912, when the observatory was bequeathed to Harvard, Blue Hill had achieved international recognition for its unique climatological record and the most complete meteorological library in the United States outside Washington, D.C.

In addition to its data-collection and instrumentation-development programs, the observatory continued Rotch's acquisition of meteorological and climatological records from around the world, including periodicals, texts, treatises, and monographs. Burhoe served as assistant to librarian Robert Stone, who shortly after joining the staff (in 1934) became interested in the library and started restoration by cataloging, arranging exchanges, and binding accumulated serials. Monthly lists of new meteorological literature, gleaned from journals that arrived at Blue Hill from all over the world, were prepared and published in the *Bulletin of the American Meteorological Society,* which was edited by Brooks. The lists generated interest, and a loan program was set up to service Society members. During the war years, when there was a strong demand for library files, Burhoe observed that by collating military and government requests he could tell where in the world military operations would be taking place.

When Brooks became director at Blue Hill in 1931, he brought with him the headquarters of the American Meteorological Society, which he had been instrumental in founding in 1919. As Brooks's secretary, Burhoe soon became involved in helping run the Society, and through his work as librarian he became acquainted with the international literature—particularly European literature—on meteorology and climatology. From worldwide inquiries for information during World War II, Burhoe saw the need for communication about the extent of this literature (Burhoe 1941, 357–61). He helped establish *Meteorological Abstracts,* which first appeared in the *Bulletin* as a regular bibliography section, and in 1950, on his proposal, became a separate periodical. At first he did most of the abstracting work, struggling to master enough of the foreign languages and journals to communicate their substance in English.

At the spring meeting in 1941, Burhoe made a special note of the rapid increase of meteorological literature. He proposed that the meeting "make a resolution to the effect that it recommends to the various meteorological institutions and scholars of America, that they cooperate toward establishment of an adequate bibliographic service for this science in this country." A resolution to this effect was adopted by the AMS and AGU [American Geophysical Union]. This was another step toward the eventual publication of the Society's *Meteorological Abstracts and Bibliography.* Two years later, Burhoe organized the publication in Spanish, of a Latin-American section of the *Bulletin* (Conover 1985, 34).

While Brooks was consulting for the military and various committees, and developing teaching programs, Burhoe helped put out extra publications to service the training needs of the military and the U.S. Weather Bureau.

During the war years membership in the Society rapidly grew, from about 1,200 in 1937 to 2,850 in 1946. Due to lack of space at the observatory, most of the office work for the Society was done at the Burhoe residence, where a small clerical staff, supervised by Burhoe's wife, was employed. With the appointment of Spengler, the new director, in 1946, the office was moved to new headquarters, and in 1947 the Burhoes resigned (Burhoe 1947, 388–90).

When the war was over and demands for information had subsided, Burhoe's interest in religion and the problems of the human condition seemed to reemerge. In a poignant autobiographical paragraph, Burhoe reflects:

From time to time I gazed out of the observatory parapet nearly 700 feet above the city of Boston. The city on a winter morn was often blotted out by what seemed to be an ink pot black smog collected under the atmospheric temperature inversion, above which we had a clear visibility to Mt. Monadnock in New Hampshire. There was symbolism in this for me, for on these occasions, whether the smog was there or not, I was not so much concerned about the meteorological phenomena or man's pollution of the air he breathes as I was about what I knew to be the widespread frustration and anguished hearts permeating the two million people, rich and poor alike, who lived in the houses and worked in the shops and offices where cruelties and misunderstandings and lack of a meaningful and viable perspective on life gave rise to the faithlessness, treachery, and despair in their hearts and visible on their faces in the subways. I knew about racial and other social underdogs, some of whom we employed. I understood the threats to life that could result from the misuse by such populations of the many new techno-logical powers from psychological to atomic. What use is scientific and technological advance for a man whose untutored wants or passions can use it only to blot out the highest values of his life?

Such thoughts pressed upon me in the years right after the war, and led to exploring the possibility for a career more fitting to the pressing needs. I began to read again outside of my field of specialization. I revived my earlier thinking and writing towards a theology, an interpretation of the sense, meaning, duty, and hope of life grounded in the realities of which I was aware existentially and intellectually (Burhoe 1964a, 10–11).

In another autobiographical passage he reflects on the impact the war, and especially the atom bomb, had on his renewal of interest in religious matters:

But my renewed concern for religious belief and the church came not from what any churches offered but from what I thought they should offer. I was moved by the plight of the world and a revelation from the sciences. The combination of the war that launched the atom bomb and grave forebodings from my first-hand observations of a wide spectrum of human society in the Boston area led me to conclude that the world at large and locally needed something with the alleged powers of the traditional religions, something to give man a new backbone of duty and hope, which had been melted or broken by the disordering forces of science and circumstance (Burhoe 1967, 2).

With the return of his old interests, Burhoe and his wife turned to the religious needs of the family. They had not been attending church for about ten years, and they searched for a Unitarian church with a good religious education program for their children. They became active in the Arlington Street Church in Boston, where Dana McLean Greeley was the minister, and Greeley became an important supporter of Burhoe's efforts to integrate religion and science.

In the 1930s Harvard had collaborated with the Massachusetts Institute of Technology on development of meteorology in Cam-bridge. Although Blue Hill had pioneered in upper-air observation by kites and balloons, the two institutions decided that M.I.T. should be the place where the new European trends in meteorological science would be developed. Meanwhile, in 1946, Burhoe had submitted his intention to resign, without having a definite new job. After considering a number of prospects, including representing a manu-facturer of high-altitude balloons to South American meteorologists and being a manager for a new plastics firm, he was contacted by the American Academy of Arts and Sciences to fill a newly created position of executive officer. Burhoe's experience in administration at the observatory and for the Society, his involvement in the scientific community, his concern for communication, and his growing experience in editing and managing publications were no doubt seen as important qualifications for the kind of work he was to do for the Academy.

ACADEMY YEARS: TESTING AND INSTITUTING THE VISION, 1947–64

The American Academy of Arts and Sciences was granted its charter of incorporation 4 May 1780 by an act of the legislature of Massachusetts. The charter read in part:

The stated end and design of the institution of the said academy is to promote and encourage the knowledge of the antiquities of America, and of the natural history of the country, and to determine the uses to which the various natural productions of the country may be applied; to promote and encourage medical discoveries; mathematical disquisitions; philosophical enquiries and experiments; astronomical, meteorological, and geographical observations; and improvements in agriculture, arts, manufactures and commerce; and, in fine, to cultivate every art and science which may tend to advance the interest, honor, dignity, and happiness of a free, independent, and virtuous people.

Modeled upon European scientific societies, the Academy was a conspicuous center for learning and intellectual leadership in the northeastern United States during most of the nineteenth century. However, with the development of modern research universities and independent research centers in the latter part of the century, the Academy became increasingly inactive and more or less an honorary society. Its initial purposes, to promote and encourage the sciences and the arts, had in large part been achieved. With the division of knowledge, specialized societies and departments were formed to promote and encourage specific areas of investigation.

Shortly after he was elected president of the Academy in 1939, astronomer Harlow Shapley and physiological psychologist Hudson Hoagland, secretary of the Academy, began a series of discussions "devoted to the consideration of the ways in which learning derived from the systematic study of Arts and Sciences can profitably influence the reorganization of civilization in the future beyond the war" (Whitehead 1942, 1). On 8 October 1941 the first address was delivered by Alfred North Whitehead, on "Statesmanship and Specialized Learning." The discussions continued for a short time, but soon petered out (Burhoe 1964b). When literary critic Howard Mumford Jones followed Shapley as president in 1944, he revived the custom of an inaugural address and chose "to speak of the present status and possible future of the American Academy of Arts and Sciences" (Jones 1944, 131–39). He traced the history of academies to expose the roots of the problems facing American society and the Academy. The theme of his address was that the division of knowledge and the multiplication of specialties had created a new opportunity for the Academy: "The multiplication of specialities has forced the specialists to come together, to exchange ideas, to study each other's techniques, even—what is anathema to the old-fashioned, hard-boiled, realistic investigator—to discuss the philosophy of what they were doing" (Jones 1944, 134–35).

Jones did not see that the search for a common language among specialists (as became the focus of the Conferences on Science, Philosophy, and Religion at Columbia University) was practicable, for it was a

call to retreat up the stream of time to simpler eras. . . . I think the problem is wrongly phrased. I should myself put it this way: that our problem is not whether a common language can be artificially reinstituted among learned men, but whether this Academy is not charged with the duty of creating a common climate of opinion. My observation is that the research spirit does not depend upon vocabulary but upon an exciting philosophy of values (Jones 1944, 137).

He ended with the recommendation that a special commission be appointed "to review and re-examine the whole structure of this ancient institution" and to propose directions for "some positive program to link together the interests of the learned and the problems of society in the years immediately to come" (Jones 1944, 138–39).

In the winter of 1945 the Academy formed a committee to study its structure and operation, with Kirtley F. Mather as chair. On 13 November 1946 the Academy met as a committee of the whole to consider recommendations of the Report of the Commission on the Present Status and Future of the Academy:

In brief, it was the thesis of the Commission that the focus of an inclusive learned society today cannot be so much on the advancement of research and knowledge in each of the many specialized disciplines as on the "humanization" of knowledge—the revealing of the significance of knowledge for the life of man. It proposed that capital should be made of the diversity of areas of scholarship represented in the Academy membership, as well as its high level, in an attempt to synthesize knowledge for the welfare of the community, particularly the New England community.

Among the recommendations of the commission was establishment of the position of executive officer to expand the Academy's activity. Reflecting on this new position, which he was selected to fill, Burhoe wrote:

In 1947, I found one of the most ideal positions possible for my concerns. . . . Its [the Academy's] officers and Council wanted me to assist committees of the Fellows of the Academy to accomplish various goals under an extension of its 1780 charter, "to cultivate every art and science, which may tend to advance the interest . . . of a . . . people." A prime goal was to update our "philosophical, moral, and political foundations" to adapt them to the conditions of a new century and of a whole world of people made interdependent by scientific technology. I was given a wonderful opportunity to work with some of the best minds in many disciplines, in programs to make sense of various human problems (Burhoe 1981, 14–15).

Although the scientists and intellectuals in the Academy were mostly secularists, they were deeply concerned with the implications of the academic syllabus for human welfare. Burhoe shared the thought, in the "smoothly rounded phrases" of the Academy's charter and early documents, "that the spirit, purpose and essential logical and instrumental methodology of science can be applied more or less readily and successfully to any and every form and aspect of human knowledge" (Burhoe 1964b, 7). He also shared the idea, expressed by Jones, that the research spirit depends upon an exciting philosophy of values. In addition, Burhoe was convinced that any discussion of values necessarily involved religion and that a climate of opinion that did not seriously consider religion would be an incomplete development. He was also convinced that religion could be shown to be essential in shaping the values of a culture and that the contemporary problem of religion was largely of an intellectual nature. He felt strongly the need of an intellectual breakthrough so that educated persons could appreciate religion and its traditional wisdom vis-à-vis ultimate values. He wrote: "Discussions with these groups of scientists more than the church became for me the center of what I call my religious and theological life. Here were ideas about reality and man that were accepted by the scientific community and which at the same time illuminated the problems of human values" (Burhoe 1949, G-8).

During his seventeen-year tenure with the Academy (1947 to 1964), Burhoe's theological ideas began to be characterized by its potent scientific and intellectual climate. He began to articulate his interpretation of religion, testing it in front of these secular and humanistically oriented intellectuals.

Thus 1947 marked an important transition in the life of Ralph Wendell Burhoe. His primary concern, to integrate religion into a secular intellectual culture, dominated by science and technology, clawed its way to the surface after years of hibernation in Blue

Hill—and he found support and encouragement in the Academy for working out his vision of religion in the light of the sciences. In his work with the Academy, Burhoe became familiar with the scientific and intellectual currents of thought, and he began to articulate his theological perspective in the Academy's terms. Indeed, his years of working with the Academy may be described as the fulfillment of his education, which had been disrupted during the Depression and the war years. Working with widely recognized leaders on the development of conferences, meetings, seminars, and publications, on a wide range of topics, gave breadth and depth to Burhoe that few, if any, graduate programs could match. This rare opportunity is reflected in the range and depth of issues that Burhoe addressed in developing his scientific theology.

Although Burhoe became immersed in managing the Academy, in 1948, in accord with new directions for its publications program, he began to edit a new *Bulletin* to communicate announcements and summaries of routine affairs of the Academy. *Proceedings* was gradually transformed into *Dædalus,* which, after experiments with a new philosophy, title, and format between 1955 and 1956, became a widely distributed quarterly under the editorship of Gerald Holton in 1957. In addition to this work, Burhoe administered a burgeoning program of committees, meetings, conferences, and seminars that implemented the vision of the Mather Report. A paragraph from his 1964 "Review and Farewell" address to the Academy indicates the scope and influence of these activities:

An inspection of what the Academy has been doing during the last couple of decades bears testimony to the fruitfulness of this vision of the Academy's role in contemporary civilization. More than a hundred special committees have brought interdisciplinary and inter-institutional, interstate, and international scholars and men of affairs together to survey, examine, evaluate, and publish their findings and recommendations in the light of their considered studies. These have ranged over the whole spectrum of intellectual and human problems, from the nature of knowledge to the prevention of atomic catastrophe. All of them have stimulated widespread developments outside the Academy, and some of them have had recognizable impact on the well-being of the people. Notable has been the impact of about ten different committees of the Academy on national and international understanding and control of nuclear arms. In Washington and London as well as in Boston I have heard the testimony of outsiders on the impact of the studies, conferences, and publications of the Academy on the climate of opinion. In Chicago a knowledgeable outsider recently volunteered that our late Fellow, John F. Kennedy, had been assisted in no small measure by the work of these Academy committees to sign an agreement with the Soviets to limit atmospheric testing of nuclear weapons (Burhoe 1964b, 7–8).

Two of many activities in his work with committees and conferences at the Academy need to be pointed out. The atom bomb and nuclear energy raised serious moral and social problems that few outside the scientific community comprehended; so "we established numerous committees to study or act in various ways to try to provide some practical salvation. We supported the nascent *Bulletin of the Atomic Scientists* in its efforts to make the governments and other leaders of the world aware of the implications of atomic energy" (Burhoe 1967, 6). However, Burhoe was not fully convinced that such deliberations, which did not take religion into account, would contribute significantly to world peace. He took seriously the problems related to nuclear war; however, he was searching for ways of approaching the problems that pondered the resources of religion.

In 1960 Hudson Hoagland was instrumental in obtaining a Carnegie Corporation grant of $150,000 to develop conferences and publications under the broad category "Life, Liberty and the Pursuit of Meaning" (Burhoe 1964b, 2).[2] At a time of renewed interest in evolutionary theory because of the centennial of the publication of Darwin's *Origin of Species,* Hoagland and Burhoe organized three conferences in the fall of 1960 on "Evolutionary Theory and Human Progress." The conferences focused on long-range trends in human evolution and sought to relate cultural to genetic evolution.

Because of their special knowledge, scientists and scholars may be in a position to see some of the future consequences and costs of current social practices before they become evident to decision makers, either in large enterprises like governments or small enterprises like families. Few have either the time or the talent to become informed about long-range implications arising from advances in science and technology. And yet in the twentieth century, as compared with previous centuries, the impact of science and technology upon our ways of living and our destiny has become paramount (Burhoe and Hoagland 1962, 1).

In 1975, reflecting on the significance of these conferences, Burhoe wrote:

My own efforts to translate religious beliefs into scientific language began when I was a preacher in 1935. Because of the lack of any audience ready to hear of such notions until I began to work with some first-rate scientists on problems of science and human values in the American Academy after World War II, I did little and published nothing until the mid 1950s. . . . In 1960, Hudson Hoagland and I sought to evoke some new thinking on the relation of cultural to biological evolution which had been an academically taboo area for a half-century. . . . These symposia were influential in a renaissance of thought and research concerning sociocultural evolution in relation to biological evolution and provided me with much critical information (Burhoe 1975, 371).

These conferences gave Burhoe encouragement and conceptual resources for the development of his evolutionary interpretation of religion. In addition, they placed his developing theory within the larger perspective of a renaissance of research into the relationship between biological and sociocultural evolution.

Three other relationships warrant discussion: Philipp Frank and the Institute for the Unity of Science, the Committee on Science and Values, and the Society for the Scientific Study of Religion—all of which began within a year or two of Burhoe's work with the Academy. The first two activities were related to the Academy with a substantial overlap of personnel, in whom Burhoe found kindred spirits concerned with ideals and seeking (in the spirit intended by Whitehead in his 1941 paper) "to apply the large generalizations of the sciences for sociological reconstruction" (Burhoe 1967, 7). The Institute for the Unity of Science sought to bridge the sciences and the humanities by a transformed philosophy of science, but it did not have a positive outlook on religious traditions. The Society for the Scientific Study of Religion (first organized as the Committee for the Scientific Study of Religion) was oriented to the psychosocial sciences and, in general, did not accept the ideas of the physical and biological sciences. The Academy's Committee on Science and Values embraced all the sciences for shedding light on the question of human values. Several members of this committee became involved in a new Institute on Religion in an Age of Science, which became the embodiment of Burhoe's vision for the revitalization of religion in the light of the sciences.

PHILIPP FRANK AND THE INSTITUTE FOR THE UNITY OF SCIENCE

Philipp Frank, a physicist whose chief interest was the philosophy of science, was one of the three most active members of a discussion group that began about 1907 in Vienna. "I used to associate with a group of students who assembled every Thursday night in one of the old Viennese coffee houses. We stayed until midnight and even later, discussing problems of science and philosophy" (Frank 1950, 1). The other two were the mathematician Hans Hahn, and the economist Otto Neurath. The problem that concerned the group was association of the failure of mechanistic physics with belief that the scientific method had failed. So intimately connected was mechanistic physics with metaphysics and the ideal of progress in science that abandonment of the nineteenth-century optimism that mechanistic physics could embrace all observations led to a number of alternatives. One could retain a commonsense metaphysics, give up faith in the scientific method, and see contemporary physics as a threat to common understanding. Or one could reject mechanistic explanations and retrieve an organismic metaphysics from the Greeks. Or one could abandon metaphysics, whether organismic or mechanistic. The latter approach was adopted by what came to be called the Vienna Circle.

The whole original Vienna group was convinced that the elimination of metaphysics not only was a question of a better logic but was of great relevance for the social and cultural life. They were also convinced that the elimination of metaphysics would deprive the groups that we call today totalitarian of their scientific and philosophic basis and would lay bare the fact that these groups were actually fighting for special interests of some kind (Frank 1950, 34).

In 1922 Hahn was instrumental in the appointment of the physicist and philosopher, Moritz Schlick, at Vienna, and in 1926 Schlick persuaded Rudolf Carnap to move to Vienna. Schlick and Carnap expanded the new positivism, which combined Ernst Mach's empiricism and symbolic logic into a general, logical basis for thought. This synthesis gave the Vienna Circle its distinctive programmatic basis for building a new philosophy. The primary philosophical problem that occupied the Vienna Circle was the relationship between the conceptual language in scientific description and the observations of empirical experience that those concepts claimed to organize, upon which their validity depended.

Growing out of the work of the Vienna Circle was a movement for a unified science (see Joergensen 1951, 76). Otto Neurath, who introduced the expression *unity of science* into logical empiricism (Joergensen 1951, 76), agreed with Rudolf Carnap that unification of the sciences should come about through formation of a universal language of science. In the 1930s a number of international congresses and publications were devoted to the examination and development of such a universal scientific language, and in 1938 the *International Encyclopedia of Unified Science* began publication (Joergensen 1951, 40–48), although the outbreak of World War II slowed progress. The Institute for the Unity of Science was founded in 1947, following the war, "to encourage the integration of knowledge by scientific methods, to conduct research in the psychological and sociological backgrounds of science" (Frank 1951, 6). The Institute was furnished quarters by the Academy, and in 1949 the Institute was incorporated as owner and director of the *Encyclopedia,* with Philipp Frank as president of the board of trustees (Joergensen 1951, 100). In the same year the Academy appointed a Committee on the Unity of Science, composed of Percy W. Bridgman (chair), Horace S. Ford and Philipp Frank, to administer a Rockefeller Foundation grant "in support of activities aimed at making more sound and effective the interrelationships between the various branches of the natural sciences, the social sciences, and the humanities"—in cooperation with the Institute. Thus at the beginning of his tenure as executive officer of the Academy, Burhoe became closely associated with Frank and the work of the Institute.

This association greatly influenced Burhoe's philosophy of science and his conviction that its universal language should be that in which religious doctrine should be reformulated, thereby leading to a universal interpretation of religion as a natural phenomenon. An important aspect of Burhoe's program of scientific theology was translation of traditional religious concepts and doctrines into the language of science (see Burhoe 1973, 438; 1975, 330, 351). (Compare this idea with Joergensen's description of Neurath's program for the unity of science.)

Carnap and Neurath soon agreed that it would be more expedient to use a physicalistic language than an egocentric, phenomenological one.

The task then became to formulate the rules of formation and of transformation of such language so that all concepts and sentences can be expressed in it, if necessary, by suitable translation and so that all scientific theories can by means of it be reduced to as few deductive systems as possible, preferably to a single one (Joergensen 1951, 77).

The motivation for a physicalistic language is best explained by Frank:

What we call in a vague way "common sense" is actually an older system of science which was dropped because new discoveries demanded a new conceptual scheme, a new language of science. Therefore the attempt to interpret scientific principles by "common sense" means actually an attempt to formulate our actual science by a conceptual scheme that was adequate to an older stage of science, now abandoned (Frank 1950, 301).

Thus one understands why Burhoe insisted that religion be interpreted in terms of the current scientific conception of the world, not the other way around, for to interpret science in terms of traditional religious concepts is to attempt to formulate scientific concepts in terms of an older, abandoned conceptual scheme that is no longer adequate.

The focus of the Institute was on developing the philosophy of science as a way toward the integration of science, philosophy, and the humanities. In the words of Philipp Frank, the philosophy of science is "the missing link between science and philosophy": To understand not only science but the place of science in our civilization, its relation to ethics, politics, and religion, we need a coherent system of concepts and laws within which the natural sciences, as well as philosophy and the humanities have their place. Such a system may be called philosophy of science,'' [sic] it would be the ''missing link'' between the sciences and the humanities without introducing any perennial philosophy that could only be upheld by authorities (Frank 1957, xv).

Burhoe's primary concern, however, was to interpret religion by using the methods and conceptual tools of the sciences. If Burhoe had been concerned with a theology of science or with establishing theology as one of the sciences, the problems engaged by a philosophy of science would no doubt have been more prominent in his thought. His intention, however, was theoretical construction, in the spirit of the sciences, of an interpretation of religion and not of science.

THE SOCIETY FOR THE SCIENTIFIC STUDY OF RELIGION

In addition to associating with Frank and his work with the Academy, Burhoe became involved with a group of social scientists who were concerned about the scientific study of religion. In 1949, J. Paul Williams (in the Department of Religion at Mount Holyoke) and Walter H. Clark (in the Department of Psychology at Middlebury College, Vermont) formed the Committee for the Social Scientific Study of Religion with the purpose of getting social scientists and religious persons together to talk about problems of religious study and to encourage research in the field. Soon joined by Prentice Pemberton (staff member of the Student Christian Movement), they gathered a number of interested scholars. Horace Kallen, Gorden Allport, James Luther Adams, Paul Tillich, Pitirim Sorokin, Talcott Parsons, Allan Eister, Lauris Whitman, and Ralph Burhoe were among the participants in the early meetings (Newman 1974, 137–51). The scientific study of religion from sociological and psychological perspectives fit with Burhoe's concern for rendering religion credible on scientific grounds.

In the early 1950s he participated in the working group with Williams, Pemberton, Clark, Kallen, Eister, and Whitman and the organization of the fledgling Society. He served as the first chair of the Committee on Research Endorsements, established in 1954, and helped organize a Midwest regional group, chaired by James Luther Adams (then of Meadville Theological School), which became a regional association of the newly named Society for the Scientific Study of Religion (the SSSR) in 1955. In 1956 he proposed that a journal be started, and he was active in the preliminary work that led to establishment of the *Journal for the Scientific Study of Religion* in 1961. He continued to be active in the affairs of the Society through the

1960s, and in 1984 Burhoe was the first recipient of the Society's Distinguished Career Achievement Award. In his remarks during its presentation, Charles Glock noted a divergence of the SSSR's perspective from that of Burhoe, whose "training is in the natural sciences and it was his hope that our Society would include a natural scientific component and involve natural scientists working alongside social scientists in the study of religion and from a perspective which would include his theoretical stance. Our Society did not move in these directions. Then and now, it would be more accurate probably to call ourselves the Society for the Social Scientific Study of Religion" (Glock 1984).

Burhoe was an occasional contributor to the deliberations of the SSSR, and in 1951 he presented a paper, "A Scientific Theory of Soul," in which he first put forth his trinitarian idea of soul. The soul has a biological component, the genotype; a cultural component (which he later called the culturetype); and a cosmic or environmental component, to which he later referred as the cosmotype. Over a lifetime, the dynamic interaction of these components produce the living phenotypic expression in a human (Burhoe 1951b, 1). In other papers, he brought his conception of the relation of science and religion into play on the topic at hand, often distinguishing his perspective from the general thrust of scholarship in the SSSR. In a 1984 paper he outlined four areas in which he diverged from the SSSR: (1) inclusion of all fields of scholarship, with a unique role for the natural sciences—rather than the more narrow focus of the SSSR on sociology and psychology; (2) appreciation for and enhancement of religion, scientifically grounded in a theory of the function of religion in biocultural evolution; (3) a paradigmatic concept of an evolving, continuous, and connected hierarchy of events in the cosmos, from atoms to human cultures, in which religion plays an important role in human evolution; and (4) reasons for eliminating the intellectual separation between scientific facts and religious values (Burhoe 1984a, 3–7).

In an article on the study of the sociology of religion, Robert Friedrichs argued that the discipline had lost its theological dimension, which he attributed to the demise of the détente between theology and the sciences that had been in effect for the past two to three generations (Friedrichs 1974, 113–27). If this is an accurate assessment, Friedrichs points to a significant divergence of the goals of the SSSR from the initial purposes that attracted Burhoe, who had always pressed for not only a scientific interpretation of religion but for its *enhancement*—the practical fruit that this interpretation would undoubtedly bear. That is to say, Burhoe has always had a theological as well as a practical interest in the scientific study of religion. Because the SSSR did not develop along these lines, Burhoe developed other options. "In any case," Glock says, "acknowledging the legitimacy of how our Society was evolving but recognizing that it was not going to satisfy fully his own aspirations for it, Burhoe decided to create institutional arrangements which would serve his purposes more effectively" (Glock 1984).

THE COMMITTEE ON SCIENCE AND VALUES

In his first year with the Academy, Burhoe discovered a group of scientists who shared his concerns about religion and science, although they considered religion (if at all) in the context of what they thought were the larger problem of human values. "To my delight, I found among the Academy Fellows a number of scientists and other scholars in diverse disciplines who were interested in understanding the nature of human values" (Burhoe 1981, 15). In 1948 Burhoe helped revive the discussions that Hudson Hoagland and Harlow Shapley had initiated in 1940 on contributions that the sciences might make to the reorganization of civilization after the war. A new group began to meet, as the Seminar on Science and Values, and in 1950 it petitioned the Academy Council to establish a Committee on Science and Values.

A statement by several Fellows petitioning for the establishment of this committee said, in part: "We believe that the sudden changing of man's physical and mental climate brought about by science and technology in the last century has rendered inadequate ancient institutional structures and educational forms, and that the survival of human society depends on a re-formulation of man's world-view and ethics, by grounding them in the revelations of modern science as well as on tradition and intuition. . . . We propose, therefore, that a Committee on Science and Values be established to encourage the study of basic individual and social needs, especially to discover what light an integrated world-view of the sciences, arts and humanities can shed upon the present historical scene. We believe this to be a crucial problem of our times and that the Academy can and should provide initiative, because it is an institution whose membership encompasses outstanding leaders in the wide range of professions concerned, because its quality is respected, and because it can afford to consider long-range and fundamental problems. Moreover, we believe that the integration and application of the departments of knowledge in this fashion to the problems of society is a most fitting interpretation for the year 1950 of the terms of our Charter of 1780 which made it plain that the purpose of the Academy was not the cultivation of knowledge for its own sake but to advance the interests of the people" (Burhoe 1951a, 4).

Academy Fellows on the new committee (which was approved and installed) included C. J. Ducasse (philosophy, Brown University), Philipp Frank (physics and philosophy, Harvard), Roy G. Hoskins (neuroendocrinology, Harvard), Henry Alexander Murray (clinical psychology, Harvard), H. B. Phillips (mathematics, M.I.T.), Laszlo Tisza (thermodynamics, M.I.T.), Robert Ulich (philosophy, Harvard University School of Education), and George Wald (biology, Harvard). The committee, because it had overlapping interests and personnel, often cooperated with the Institute for the Unity of Science in sponsoring seminars and meetings.

In 1952 this committee began a series of events that eventuated in establishing the Institute on Religion in an Age of Science (IRAS):

At a meeting on 8 May 1952 under the chairmanship of biochemist George Wald, committee members agreed, "because of the importance of religion to our social structure," we should share some of the newer and better interpretations of the implications of the sciences for religion with clergy who expressed an interest (Burhoe 1981, 15).[3]

Earlier—probably in 1951—the committee had received a compilation, "Questions to the Scientist from the Clergy" by Dana McLean Greeley, Burhoe's minister at Arlington Street Church, that expressed the interest of a number of clergy in a dialogue with scientists (see Greeley 1971).

THE COMING GREAT CHURCH CONFERENCES

Greeley had suggested that Burhoe attend a conference, on "The Coming Great Church," in the summer of 1952. The conference, which had been meeting since 1950 at Star Island in the Isles of Shoals off Portsmouth, New Hampshire, was "dedicated to the proposition that an opportunity should be provided for religious leaders to lift their discussion above the narrow boundaries of creed, dogma, or denomination into the realm of common understanding" (Rutledge 1951, ix). In his recollections on "Adventures in Ecumenicity," Greeley described the origin and nature of the conference:

The Reverend Lyman V. Rutledge had the idea first, I guess. He was joined by the Reverend Robert Illingworth—that meant a Unitarian and a Congregationalist—and they enrolled Professor Edwin Prince Booth, a very liberal Methodist, and me in the effort to create a new conference on "The Coming Greater Church." This had to do with the vision of a united or nonsectarian inclusive church, or with what would be called today truly ecumenical dialogue and fellowship. Conferences were held for four summers, after which they evolved under the same management into a second emphasis in a subsequent series of conferences, "Religion in an Age of Science." And from the latter were born both a denominational commission of the Unitarian Universalist Association and finally a department of the Meadville Theological School of Chicago. The initiation of the conference on "The Coming Greater Church" was surely an adventure in

ecumenicity. It led in a truly pioneering fashion to the presence of representatives not only of many denominations but also of major faiths—
Protestantism, Catholicism, Judaism, and Hinduism—in one hallowed
spot, with daily Catholic masses as well as the traditional liberal candlelight
services being held in the little two-century-old chapel (Greeley 1971, 200).

Booth, who had studied under Adolf von Harnack and was
professor of historical theology at Boston University, spoke on the
intent of the conferences in his chapel talks:

Most of us recognize that a greater church must come if the church is to
endure. In this recognition we have no disloyalty to the past. Nor do we
show any lack of allegiance to the present organizations in which we hold our
memberships. We simply recognize that a new world situation surrounds us
in every avenue of life. For the meeting of this mighty challenge the church
must adapt herself. It is *coming*. It will be *great*. And it will still be the *church*.
Therefore, we commit ourselves to consider the Coming Great Church. . . .
It is my main thesis that we have come to such a point historically in all lines
of endeavor that no organization we have inherited from the past is equal to
the direction of the present or the charting of the future. . . . The present
church, I think, is inadequate for the task required of the religious spirit.
[Because its present, fragmented structure is] modeled upon the historical
framework of long ago. . . . The Christian church must be prepared to lose
its present life in order to gain a true spiritual life. . . . It is a Christian
Theistic Humanism for which I call. Its basic affirmation is that God is the
creator of this and all other universe, that He is revealed to us in history
under the highest form of life we know—personal! (Booth 1951, 1, 6, 9, 50).

Earlier in the same talk, Booth had called for "the Coming Great
Church":

Upon a universalized basis which admits the presence of the living God in
non-Christian religions as well as in Christian; upon a basis of truth for
which the teachings of science are the guide; upon the centrality of the Jesus
of history in interpreting the purposes of God; upon the affirmation that God
has new light for each succeeding stage in civilization—upon these the
Coming Great Church must be built (Booth 1951, 10–11).

Although science was perceived as important for the "Coming
Great Church," the deliberations of the conference centered around
religious and theological issues, "because the conference involved
only the people and the ideas within the religious traditions, and
largely overlooked the relevance for religion of the newer interpretations of reality by the light of modern science" (Brown 1963). Booth
had said: "The truths discovered by science are of such a nature that
they invalidate many of the theological presuppositions of the past,
and call for a thorough-going restatement of Christianity" (Booth
1951, 9); therefore Burhoe saw an opening for introducing his
concerns for the integration of religion and science. During the 1952

conference he gave an impromptu review of Richard von Mises's recently translated *Positivism: A Study in Human Understanding* (Mises 1951), in which von Mises sought "to show how, in contrast to Wittgenstein, positivism's paradigm could encompass and enlighten our understanding of human values" (Burhoe 1984b). Burhoe suggested to Booth and other leaders of the conference that if they wanted to consider the teachings of science a guide, the involvement of some members of the Academy Committee on Science and Values could be arranged (Burhoe 1978, 36). Because of this suggestion and the idea that science could shed light on the problems of religion and fundamental human values, and hence lead to a credible and revitalized religion, Burhoe in the fall of 1953 was invited to plan a conference for the summer of 1954 on the theme "Religion in the Age of Science."

Burhoe arranged a program of fifteen papers by scientists, philosophers, and theologians, and some extracts from his report on the conference (for *Science*) give the tenor of the conference:

Ten scientists explained how they thought scientific and religious knowledge could be integrated. . . . Called in the faith that the understanding of religious "truth and reality" is related to the understanding of scientific "truth and reality," the conference stimulated considerable discussion concerning the nature of scientific "truth." . . . While there were a number of both scientists and clergymen who held that religious truth was hardly susceptible to being approached by scientific methods, except perhaps in the negative sense of being prohibited by scientific beliefs, there was a strong and seemingly growing recognition that today man can increase the scope and validity of his understanding of his destiny and of his relationship to that "in which he lives and moves and has his being," not only by reading ancient texts, but also by building up the science of theology in harmony with other science. . . .

The new strategy, suggested by many from both the camp of science and the camp of religion in this peace conference in the cold war between science and religion, is that theology should no longer stake its claims in the area where science is ignorant, but rather that theology should accept and integrate with developments of the several branches of knowledge represented by the sciences. . . .

The general tone of the conference throughout was one of cooperative cordiality and even elation. . . The clergy and lay members of the conference were deeply impressed with the grand sweep of knowledge about man and his destiny in terms of the scientific view of the universe. . . .

Many came away with a deeper understanding of what Pope Pius XII may have meant when he said to the Pontifical Academy of Science, 22 Nov 1951: "In fact, according to the measure of its progress, and contrary to affirmations advanced in the past, true science discovers God in an ever-increasing degree—as though God were waiting behind every door opened by science." There were suggestions that more specific cooperation should be developed between scientists and theologians. It was proposed that interdisciplinary seminars be established to develop modern moral and religious doctrine in the light of science and that all relevant branches of science should be represented in theological school faculties. There was widespread confidence that the conference had opened a way to an integration of religion and science that would indeed provide a more hopeful basis for cooperation and satisfactory living on the part of man in an age of science (Burhoe 1954).

In the fall of 1954 Burhoe drafted a "Statement of Purpose" for a new Institute on Religion in an Age of Science at the request of a Steering Committee composed of Carl Bihldorf, Edwin P. Booth, Burhoe, Dana McLean Greeley, and Lyman V. Rutledge, all of whom (except Burhoe) had been organizers of the Coming Great Church Conferences. The statement was carefully written in consultation with the committee and others associated with the Academy Committee on Science and Values. On 9 November 1954 the Coming Great Church Conference Committee voted to "resolve itself into the 'Institute on Religion in an Age of Science' " (Burhoe 1978, 36). The following is the statement of purpose, which served until a constitution was adopted (on 5 May 1956). (Most of the statement was included in Burhoe's report on the 1955 Star Island Conference in *Science*.)[4]

The Institute on Religion in an Age of Science is established to promote creative efforts leading to the formulation, in the light of contemporary knowledge, of more effective doctrines and practices for human salvation. Its immediate function is to provide a broader and more adequate management to carry on the work initiated by the Conference on Religion in an Age of Science, held on Star Island, off Portsmouth, New Hampshire, July 31 to August 6, 1954. The basic purpose of the Institute stems from a recognition of the confusion and inadequacies of the world's many competing religions and philosophies.

The program of the Institute proceeds in the faith that there is no wall isolating any department of human understanding, and that, therefore, any doctrine of human salvation cannot successfully be separated from realities pictured by science. We believe that science provides rich new insights into the problems of human welfare and offers the possibility of a reformulation of the doctrines about the nature of man and about the nature of that in which he lives and moves and has his being. We think any scientifically substantiated notions may command wider acceptance and provide more effective programs of living for both the individual and society. We believe that any department of human knowledge may yield important contributions, including the physical, biological, and psychological sciences, as well as all fields of scholarship and interpretation of human culture.

We suspect that, in this search for a clear and modern statement of human values, much of what has been revealed by the great religious teachers of the past will stand forth in new brightness and detail, although we welcome any clearing away of misunderstandings or inadequate doctrines about the nature of reality and values. Certainly, for our times as for any time in the past, it seems that the first and most important task of man is to discover the highest values of his own nature and to orient himself properly with respect to the requirements placed upon his development by the complex and many-dimensioned cosmos.

It is proposed that the Institute operate summer conferences, carrying forward the work of our 1954 Conference on Religion in an Age of Science, and engage in the development of such additional conferences, study groups, seminars, publications, research projects, etc., as may be useful for its purposes. It is proposed that the Institute's program be defined by a Board of Advisors (limited to 50) and carried out by a Board of Directors or Executive Committee (limited to 9).

It was into this new Institute (IRAS) that Burhoe poured a substantial part of his spare time, for he realized it was a vehicle for the religious and theological angst that had been gnawing at his heart since the 1930s: to revitalize religion in the light of the sciences. Although his primary responsibilities lay with his job at the Academy, and many developments in the Academy are of import for understanding his intellectual development, Burhoe's life from 1954 onward began to blossom, inextricably intertwined with the developments at IRAS, the Institute on Religion in an Age of Science.

NOTES

1. In 1927 Buchman referred to the movement as The First Century Christian Fellowship. In 1928 it assumed the name The Oxford Group, given during a South African evangelism tour. Following a speech by Buchman on 29 May 1938, it became known as the Moral Re-Armament Movement (the MRA). However, many of its detractors referred to it as the Buchmanite movement.

2. Hoagland in Burhoe, 13 May 1964. Burhoe was heavily involved with Hoagland in developing the first of these conferences in 1960, which sought to explore "bridges" between biological and cultural evolution. In 1962 a six-week program at Craigville on Cape Cod, conducted by fourteen representatives of the behavioral sciences concerned with peace research and alternatives to nuclear war in the expression of aggression, led to the publication in June 1964 of *International Conflict and Behavioral Science: The Craigville Papers,* edited by Roger Fisher. The grant also supported conferences and publications on "Utopias" in 1964 and social implications resulting from developments in the behavioral sciences in 1965.

3. It is also of note that a number of persons associated with the Committee on Science and Values, including Hudson Hoagland, Harlow Shapley, and Philipp Frank, had also participated in the Conferences on Science, Philosophy, and Religion initiated in the 1930s by Rabbi Louis Finkelstein of the Jewish Theological Seminary in New York.

4. The first and the last paragraphs are from Burhoe's transcript of the initial draft, dated Boston, 9 November 1954. The middle two paragraphs are from Burhoe 1955.

REFERENCES

Booth, Edwin Prince. 1951. *The Greater Church of the Future.* Boston: Beacon Press.

Brooks, Charles F. 1937. "Secretary's Report, 1936." *Bulletin of the American Meteorological Society* 18: 4.

Brown, Sanborn C. 1963. *Institute on Religion in an age of Science: A Ten-Year View, 1953–1963.* Boston: Institute on Religion in an Age of Science.

Burhoe, R. W. 1941. "Bibliographic Tools for Meteorological Research." Paper read at Washington meeting of the American Meteorological Society, April 1941. In *Bulletin of the American Meteorological Society* 22 (November): 357-61.

———. 1945. "Notes on Finding a Representative Snowfall Measurement." *Bulletin of the American Meteorological Society* 26 (October): 341-42.

———. 1947. "Appendix A: Report of the Retiring Business Manager, Mr. Ralph W. Burhoe." *Bulletin of the American Meteorological Society* 28 (October): 388-90.

———. 1949. "Report of the Executive Officer to the President." *Proceedings of the American Academy of Arts and Sciences* 77: 366-70.

———. 1951a. "Notes." *Bulletin of the American Academy of Arts and Sciences* 4 (May): 4.

———. 1951b. "A Scientific Theory of Soul." Paper presented at a meeting of the Committee on Social Scientific Study of Religion, Emerson Hall, Harvard University, 21 April.

———. 1954. "Religion in an Age of Science." *Science* 120 (October 1): 522-24.

———. 1955. "Religion in an Age of Science." *Science* 122 (December 30): 1277-78.

———. 1964a. "A Theological Autobiography." Paper for Meadville Faculty Seminar, 6 November.

———. 1964b. "A Review and Farewell." Communication presented to the Academy at its 184th Annual Meeting, 13 May. Boston: American Academy of Arts and Sciences.

———. 1967. "Science and World Religious Consensus." Paper for Meadville colloquy, 20 April.

———. 1973. "The Concepts of 'God' and 'Soul' in a Scientific View of Human Purpose." *Zygon: Journal of Religion & Science* 8 (September–December): 412-42.

———. 1975. "The Human Prospect and the 'Lord of History.' " *Zygon: Journal of Religion & Science* 10 (September): 299-375.

———. 1978. "The Institute on Religion in an Age of Science Joins the CSR." *Bulletin of the Council on the Study of Religion* 9 (April): 35-39.

———. 1981. *Toward a Scientific Theology.* Dublin: Christian Journals.

———. 1982. Tape-recorded conversation with David R. Breed, 26 August.

———. 1984a. "War and Peace Viewed from the Biocultural Evolution of Religion." Paper presented at Thirty-fifth Annual Meeting of the Society for Scientific Study of Religion on 28 October in Chicago.

———. 1984b. Memo from Ralph W. Burhoe on purposes of IRAS, 15 November.

———. 1985. Tape-recorded conversation with David R. Breed, 8 January.

———. 1987a. Memo to David R. Breed, 29 July.

———. 1987b. Conversation with David R. Breed, 11 August.

Burhoe, R. W., and Hudson Hoagland, eds. 1962. *Evolution and Man's Progress.* New York: Columbia Univ. Press.

Cannon, Walter B. 1932. *The Wisdom of the Body.* New York: Norton.

Clark, Walter Houston. 1951. *The Oxford Group: Its History and Significance.* New York: Bookman Associates.

Conover, John H. 1985. "Highlights of the History of the Blue Hill Observatory and the Early Days of American Meteorological Association." *Bulletin of the American Meteorological Society* 66 (January): 30-37.

Eister, Allan W. 1950. *Drawing Room Conversion: A Sociological Account of the Oxford Group Movement.* Durham, NC: Duke Univ. Press.

Frank, Philipp, 1950. *Modern Science and Its Philosophy.* Cambridge, MA: Harvard Univ. Press.

———. 1951. "Introductory Remarks" to National Conference of the Institute for the Unity of Science, April 1950, Boston. *Proceedings of the American Academy of Arts and Sciences* 80: 6.

————. 1957. *Philosophy of Science: The Link between Science and Philosophy.* Englewood Cliffs, NJ: Prentice-Hall.

Friedrichs, Robert W. 1974. "Social Research and Theology: End of Detente?" *Review of Religious Research* 15 (Spring): 113–27.

Glock, Charles Y. 1984. Remarks by Charles Y. Glock presenting the Society for the Scientific Study of Religion's Distinguished Career Achievement Award to Ralph Wendell Burhoe on 27 October 1984, Chicago, during the Society's thirty-fifth annual meeting [copy of typewritten manuscript].

Greeley, Dana McLean. 1971. *25 Beacon Street and Other Recollections.* Boston: Beacon Press.

Hooten, Earnest Albert. 1931. *Up from the Ape.* New York: Macmillan.

Joergensen, Joergen. 1951. *The Development of Logical Empiricism.* Chicago: Univ. of Chicago Press.

Jones, Howard Mumford. 1944. "Presidential Address: The Future of the Academy." *Proceedings of the American Academy of Arts and Sciences* 75 (December): 131–39.

Kuklick, Bruce. 1977. *The Rise of American Philosophy: Cambridge, Massachusetts 1860–1930.* New Haven: Yale Univ. Press.

Mises, Richard von. 1951. *Positivism: A Study in Human Understanding.* Cambridge, MA: Harvard Univ. Press.

Newman, William M. 1974. "The Society for the Scientific Study of Religion: The Development of an Academic Society." *Review of Religious Research* 15 (Spring): 137–51.

Rutledge, Lyman V. 1951. Foreword to *The Greater Church of the Future* by Edwin Prince Booth. Boston: Beacon Press.

Whitehead, A[lfred]. N[orth]. 1942. "Statesmanship and Specialized Learning." *Proceedings of the American Academy of Arts and Sciences* 75: 1–5.

II Formulating the Vision and Organizing the Institute on Religion in an Age of Science (IRAS)

In the previous chapter I traced Burhoe's life to the founding of the Institute on Religion in an Age of Science (IRAS), which joined the Conference on the Coming Great Church and persons associated with the American Academy's Committee on Science and Values in 1955. With the establishment of IRAS, Burhoe began the development of a scientific theology, and until he resigned his position with the Academy in 1964, the record of his thought is largely (though not exclusively) contained in his memos, correspondence, reports, and proposals for conferences and other IRAS projects. Burhoe served as IRAS secretary-treasurer from the group's beginning until 1961, and as chairman of its Program Committee from 1953 (when he was asked to plan the first conference) to 1958, when he resigned and was appointed chairman of a new Publication Committee and editor of a proposed quarterly journal (IRAS 1958d, 1958e). In July 1957, he was designated Executive Secretary (IRAS 1957a) and in 1961 he was elected Honorary President for Life in recognition of his service and leadership. During the formative years of the Institute, Burhoe was the primary author of most of the documents that guided its programs and recorded its affairs. In fact, the formulation of his position, which he published in "Salvation in the Twentieth Century" in 1960, was the result of a conversation with "intellectual architects" of "a fruitful program for integrating religion and science" (Burhoe 1956b). There can be little doubt that IRAS was the primary source of inspiration, critique, and testing for the formulation of Burhoe's thought as well.

Almost from its beginning, IRAS focused on four components: (1) conferences and seminars, (2) a publications program, (3) lectures and seminars at colleges and theological schools, and (4) a center for research and advanced study. Since its beginning, moreover, its annual conference on Star Island has been central, along with seminars arranged with other groups. Whereas the first section of this chapter deals with Burhoe's vision in the context of IRAS, the second section deals with the development of seminars at theological schools, which led to the involvement of Burhoe and some IRAS members with a Unitarian commission for assessing the free church in a changing world, out of which developed a Department of Theology and the Frontiers of Learning, a center for advanced study, and the journal *Zygon* (at Meadville/Lombard Theological School in Chicago). Accordingly, this chapter concludes with a discussion of Burhoe's vision for integrating religion and science as the program was formulated in 1960.

ORGANIZATION OF THE INSTITUTE

During the 1955 Star Island conference (30 July to 6 August), when IRAS was organized, twenty-two "leading contributors to the thinking of the conferences were elected to the governing board of the institute" (Burhoe 1955). Three scientists were part of the Steering Committee, rounding out an Executive Committee of eight. During the following year, on 5 May 1956, the members approved a constitution and bylaws, and the Institute was incorporated. Its Advisory Board, which until 1959 was the entire membership, made recommendations to a Council of twelve members who conducted the affairs and business of the Institute. In the first years, Edwin Prince Booth served as president; Burhoe was secretary-treasurer; and Harlow Shapley was vice president and chairman of the Advisory Board.

In addition to almost daily meetings during the week-long summer conferences on Star Island, the Advisory Board met several times during the academic year in the Boston area, usually at luncheons or dinners at the Harvard Club, the Harvard Faculty Club, or the House of the Academy, and often featured a famous speaker and discussions. For example, Paul Tillich and John Dillenberger were guests at meetings during the 1955–56 academic year. The Council often met at the conclusion of a board meeting, but when there was extensive business to discuss, the Council occasionally convened at a member's home. After Burhoe went to Chicago in 1964, the Boston meetings of the Advisory Board ended and its function was absorbed by the Council, which then met once or twice during the year in addition to the meetings at Star Island. On 29 July 1970 the bylaws were changed to reflect this operation, eliminating the Board and expanding the Council in number and function.

The primary activity of the Institute, and the only one mandated in the bylaws, is the annual Star Island summer conference—on a rocky 40-acre island in the Isles of Shoals, about ten miles out from Portsmouth, New Hampshire. In the 1600s it was an English fishing village and port, and its highest point is crowned by a stone meeting-house, built in 1800. In the mid–nineteenth century a resort hotel was built, as the isle was a favorite summer colony for artists and writers. At the turn of the century, while the island's resort business declined, it was replaced by a growing program of Unitarian and Congregational summer conferences, and in 1915 the island was purchased by a group of Unitarians and Congregationalists as a religious conference center. In *IRAS: A Ten-Year View*, Sanborn Brown wrote about the first IRAS conferences: "It was the plan at first to enter the quest [of the meaning of science for morals and religion] from the religious frame of reference by using the traditions of Star Island in morning Chapel and evening 'candlelight' services as well as lectures and discussions. Within this environment the men of the sciences set forth, lecture by lecture, and day by day, the findings of the areas of investigation committed to them" (Brown 1963, 5). The morning started with a chapel service, at which Edwin Booth was usually the preacher, followed by a lecture and discussion. In the early afternoon the Advisory Board often met, followed by special colloquia, and in the evening there was another lecture and discussion, followed by a candlelight chapel service (which continued a tradition dating back to the first settlers). Then, in an "Owl Session," Harlow Shapley presided over an informal discussion called The Hollow Square. Thus the Star Island conferences provided a rich and intensive intellectual and spiritual experience, which is still at the center of the Institute's program. Indeed, the Institute fostered a dialogue out of which came a new paradigm for integrating religion and science, and Burhoe, as the scribe at the center of this dialogue, came to embody this emerging paradigm in both his person and thought.

PURPOSES OF THE INSTITUTE

IRAS was established "to promote creative efforts leading to the formulation, in the light of contemporary knowledge, of more effective doctrines and practices for human salvation." Beginning with the election of the first members in 1955, elaboration of this statement was the focus of meetings of the Advisory Board and the Council. Among the first concerns was a journal to integrate religion and science, employing the highest scholarly and scientific integrity, and an early discussion indicates the approach: "We viewed religions as cultural products whose evolutionary selections guaranteed [all] values in them, and we viewed science not as a substitute but as a means of clarifying and supplementing the existing religions. But we would not look for unlikely scientific confirmations of abandoned cosmologies and concepts . . . but would seek to understand the more fundamental values described in terms of those cosmologies and look to see whether and how current cosmologies support or modify them'' (IRAS 1956a). In a proposal for the 1956 Star Island conference on "Goodness and Motivation in 'the Light of Evolution,'" Burhoe formulated a summary of agreements, reached by IRAS leaders, that was distributed at the 25 January 1956 meeting:

In the summers of 1954 and 1955 the Conference reached considerable agreement that religion can and must be approached rationally, even scientifically. We roughly defined religion as man's effort to orient himself in his total environment. In biological language this might be translated as: man's effort to adapt to the conditions which the environment demands for life. We have presented the idea that the laws of the cosmos discovered by science are not separable from what has been meant by God's laws. In the summer of 1956 we plan to examine this scientific picture of that in which we live and move and have our being, and to search for meaning and for hope for human life—a story of salvation.

Two major questions will concern us:
A. What can modern knowledge say about goodness—values for life?
B. What can modern knowledge say about motivating man to do the good? (IRAS 1956a).

Two questions in the proposal indicate the approach to religion:

Insofar as we define religion as that aspect of a culture bearing the more generalized and integrated forms of its values, how far can we expect rational analysis and development of religion on the basis of the new knowledge to provide improvements in world civilization in ways analogous to those responsible for the improvements in transportation and communications? . . . Defining religion as that aspect of culture wherein one finds the highest or most inclusive generalization of values or goals for men to seek, how effective are the religious institutions in motivating relevant behavior? (IRAS 1956a, 4, 7).

The good or "highest" value was formulated:

We shall suppose that goodness for humans means life; that badness means death. Probably this statement is too simple, but let it stand for something to be amplified. . . . The finding of life and avoidance of death are central in much of religious literature.

Let us look to see what science says about life and how life is achieved. . . . We shall also look at the scientific picture of what makes for life and more abundant life for the individual. Perhaps here we shall find the pathway to our salvation, our highest life (IRAS 1956a, 1).

The program for the 1956 summer conference shows that the initial proposal was transformed to address this question: "In the light of the description of the universe and life which the scientists are now giving us, what content can we ascribe to the words 'good' and 'evil'?" Additionally, the program describes some beliefs of the founders:

It seems clear that science and scholarship have laid the groundwork for tremendously significant advances in our understanding of man, of the source of his being, and of the requirements laid upon him if he is to live and evolve to a higher life. We suspect that new religious doctrines based on these revelations will not destroy the values achieved by our religious inheritance any more than the new doctrines of Einstein destroy the value of the Newtonian or Archimedean doctrines of physics. If the progress of science and the history of man thus far be any guide, we suppose that the reformation should unite the religious doctrines of all people into a single evolving system of beliefs continuous with the evolving doctrines of human knowledge or sciences in general. . . .

Many of us suppose that a positive body of belief about the more ultimate values is essential to civilization, and that the revelations from science should be and can be usefully integrated with it. . . . A review of the list of Conference Members or a short conversation with a few of them will reveal that there are gathered on Star Island . . . a company of high and varied talent who for the most part are seriously dedicated to the search for useful and acceptable religious doctrine that fits both the world view of science and the moral requirements for a viable human society and a satisfying personal life (IRAS 1956c, 3-4).

This declaration echoed the "purpose statement" of the constitution adopted 5 May 1956:

The Institute on Religion in an Age of Science is established to promote creative efforts leading to the formulation, in the light of contemporary knowledge, of effective doctrines and practices for human welfare; to formulate dynamic and positive relationships between the concepts developed by science and the goals and hopes of man expressed through religion; to state human values in such universal and valid terms that they may be understood by all men whatever their cultural background and experience, in such a way as to provide a basis for world-wide cooperation (IRAS 1956b).

During the conference, Advisory Board meetings focused on the purposes and program of IRAS, and by the end of the week agreement was reached on a five-point recommendation to the Council for elaboration into a proposal for funding foundations:

(1) Establish a journal on religion in an age of science of high scholarly and scientific level.
(2) Establish a center of advanced studies on religion in an age of science.
(3) Undertake a program of meetings and conferences, led by teams from our membership at various universities and other centers to establish cooperative contact with other persons already working in kindred ways, and to find or stimulate new work.
(4) Establish a popular magazine in due course to carry to a broader public, including clergymen, religious and other educators, the better established contributions of science to a reinterpretation of man's religious traditions.

(5) Explore the possibilities of working with theological and other schools on [a] curriculum relating religion and science (IRAS 1956d).

In a report for *Science,* Burhoe wrote that the conference concurred on the basic program of the Institute:

There has been established a rather unique concurrence on the part of professional people from a wide range of the spectra of both science and theology on a fruitful program for integrating religion and science. . . .

This concurrence on a basic approach to the problem of religion in an age of science can perhaps be stated as follows. Knowledge of good and evil or of values or of man's ultimate concerns—that is, the area of religious doctrine—is considered to be essentially one with, and inseparable from, all other knowledge and to be capable of extension and correction in the same ways. This does not mean that our acquisition of knowledge (about ethics or the nature and destiny of man) is limited to knowledge gained by recent scientific methods; but it does not exclude them. Science, in short, is a part of the process by means of which valid information about man's highest concerns is revealed to him. Because of the very rapid current advance of scientific knowledge and the patently growing incompatibilities of various religious doctrines, the conference members, for the most part, seem to feel the need for a restatement of religion.

At the same time, there seems to be among the members of the conference the scientist's respect for the facts of religion and religious institutions. These are looked upon as evolved structures or patterns of human culture having the same kind of validity and usefulness in supporting life as do other evolutionary structures. And there is also a scientist's hope that one can find beneath the seemingly paradoxical and irrational phenomena of religion some kind of rational conceptual scheme to account for them. . . .

It is also a positive and new approach, since even in the heyday of religious liberalism during the earlier part of the present century, there seems to have been no comparable coming together of scientists at the invitation of religious professionals to reconsider religious doctrine for a new age (Burhoe 1956b).

As indicated by these excerpts, those who formed the initial core of IRAS reached substantial agreement on a number of operating premises, which can be summarized as follows. The primary concepts are truth, value, and religion as seen in a scientific view of the world. Science and what characterizes the scientific worldview, namely evolution, form the new light in which to see old and new observable facts. To be scientific is to be concerned with truth or matters of objective fact. Religion and science are concerned about the same truth, although it may be formulated differently. This truth, at which both science and religion aim, is empirically verifiable—that is, is open to objective scrutiny. This means that the criterion for a valid truth is scientific verification. That an ancient authority has made some claim about truth may have been of vital importance, and even correct, but for that truth to be credible today its scientific validation is essential.

These purposes suggest that the scientists in the Academy's Committee on Science and Values joined the clergy associated with the conference on the Coming Great Church out of religious affinity (see Breed, *Zygon* September 1990). Both were seeking a scientifically respectable forum for religious concerns. In particular, the scientists wanted a forum in which they could explore religious life without sacrificing their integrity; in short, they were seeking a way of being religious in a scientific way. They knew that being religious in this way was not widely acceptable among either their colleagues or their former religious communities and for the same reason: being religious meant a form of life based on the authority of a religious tradition. This was abhorrent for scientific intellectuals because it introduced criteria that were unacceptable and perspectives on world realities that were incredible, having been transformed by developments in the sciences. For the religious, on the other hand, traditional forms of the devout life were the only forms that preserved religious integrity. The IRAS founders, nonetheless, were deeply religious, in the broadest sense of the word, and were seeking new forms of religious expression that would not sacrifice their intellectual and scientific commitments. Thus the burning question was how to be religious scientifically, and this entailed exploring and testing new forms of religious life that took traditional forms of religion, as well as science, seriously. The founders wanted to find a form of life that integrated their religious feelings and their scientific rationality with the wisdom of religious traditions and the worldview revealed by the sciences and thereby find a new orientation to the total environment. Thus their concern was to formulate effective doctrines and practices for human welfare.

"Proposal for Development of Program"

On 14 September 1956 Burhoe sent his "Proposal for Development of Program" to all IRAS members for discussion at a meeting on 2 October (Burhoe 1956a). Of particular interest for this study is the rationale he developed:

1. [IRAS] seeks funds to initiate a fundamental program to formulate dynamic and positive relationships between the concepts developed by science and the goals and hopes of man expressed through religion. . . .

2. Religion is regarded as that element of human culture which forms man's attitudes towards the forces within and around him on which his life depends, attitudes whose function is to provide ultimately successful adaptation or adjustment with respect to these forces. Religious knowledge is knowledge about those areas of man's ultimate concern.

3. In the light of anthropological and sociological studies it is presumed that each of the world's religions embodies valid and useful doctrines and practices which have evolved in the experience of its respective culture. . . .

4. It is further presumed that, just as constructive aids to agriculture or medicine in the light of science have been welcomed in every culture and given man greater opportunities in these areas of life, so also will be welcomed scientific aids to religion.

5. However, in the evolution of Christian or Western civilization, the impact of science and technology . . . has increasingly tended to dissolve the faith of the educated leaders of that civilization in the great Christian conceptual scheme of values and sanctions. . . . Thus, historically, science would seem to be lethal to religious institutions. . . .

7. Probably an adequate reformulation of value doctrine can be made only by retaining the essential wisdom and truth of the old, reinterpreted in the light of science. . . . [That is,] the logical equivalence . . . of their substantial values. . . .

8. [Burhoe posits a fundamental requirement for a religion or doctrine of values.] Moreover, we believe that this approach can give religious doctrines the possibility of evolving as flexibly as the doctrines of science in general so as to conform with newly observed elements of human experience. . . .

10. In other words, if a part of a culture is determined by science, then if it is to survive it would seem its value concepts must incorporate that scientific world view. . . .

55. [IRAS] finds fruitful contributions to religion from all areas of science. From the physical sciences it finds bases for a revised epistemology, ontology, and cosmology; and from the biological and social sciences (including history) a clarified picture of the nature of man and the evolution of his doctrines of salvation. . . .

57. In general, we hold . . . that science in its most critical character does not demolish belief in a reality outside of man which he must come to know and obey if he is to have life, but establishes such a reality more firmly and truly than ever before was possible. What has been lacking has been a successful effort on the part of scientific explorers to interpret this new revelation of the reality in a way that shows its moral and religious relevance (Burhoe 1956a, 2 and passim).

These ideas engendered vigorous discussion over the next months, and these discussions, in turn, prompted Burhoe to present another proposal for the upcoming (1957) Star Island conference. He focused on the nature of truth as a way of addressing dissension and moving toward consensus among IRAS members. Moreover, we find in this proposal Burhoe's view of truth as an evolution of knowledge about right and wrong. This view can best be shown by outlining the topics to be covered at the Star Island conference:

1. Knowledge through the genotype/Genetically derived knowledge, or the wisdom of the body
2. Knowledge by perception/Perceived knowledge, or the revelation of the senses
3. Knowledge by intuition or imagination/Intuited knowledge, or revelation from beyond the senses
4. Knowledge through the mores and myths of culture/Culturally transmitted knowledge, or the revelation of the tradition
5. Knowledge from deductive reasoning or logic/Logically deduced knowledge, or the revelation of reason
6. Knowledge through science/Science, or revelation by a systematic involvement of all of the above

This general scheme served as the structure of his paper, "Five Steps in the Evolution of Man's Knowledge of Good and Evil" (Burhoe 1967).

"A STEP TOWARD A SCIENTIFIC THEOLOGY"

Burhoe's assessment of the 1957 conference is indicated by the title of his unpublished report, "A Step Toward a Scientific Theology" (Burhoe 1957). Indeed, by concentrating on methodological problems, the conference generated a harmonious consensus on how the Institute should proceed in developing its program, for by the end of the conference the Council had adopted these resolutions:

(1) to continue Star Island Conferences;
(2) to schedule lectures and conferences on the theme of the Institute wherever opportunity may be afforded;
(3) to hold one or more winter conferences annually in the Boston area;
(4) to publish a bulletin or news sheet to carry ideas pertinent to the Institute's interests;
(5) to undertake other projects as experience may suggest and as are in harmony with the aims of the Institute. . . . [And] to designate Ralph Burhoe Executive Secretary of the Institute and to provide assistance to implement the above program (IRAS 1957b).

Thus, insofar as agreement on a program was reached, a step toward a scientific theology *was* taken.

Burhoe's report underscores issues that are amplified in his later writings, such as background questions of the conference. How is it that we human beings know what we know? In particular, how do we know what is good for us and what is bad? How did we come to have moral and religious understanding? What are the sources of our information? How is truth or valid information revealed to man? What distinguishes the scientific method of getting valid information and what are its potential roles in providing answers to religious questions? (IRAS 1957a; Burhoe 1957).

A basic supposition was that decisions about the validity of beliefs or claims to truth are based on empirical evidence, and on this common ground there appears to be no difference between scientific and religious discernment of the validity of a belief. When the question as to the source of new revelations was asked, Anton Boisen said that "the rise of new concepts from out of the unknown into the conscious mind seems to be a process not essentially different in the natural sciences from that in religious and in psychotic experience" (Burhoe 1957).

Scientific and religious knowing were distinguished at two points. First, "Religious knowing was felt to differ from scientific knowing not so much because of its greater emotional or aesthetic charge, but because of its greater universality and greater sense of its significance for the ultimate goals of man." Second, by the way in which the validity of new ideas is tested. For religious knowledge or belief to be scientific entails at least making its concepts coherent within the framework of the concepts of science or objective knowledge (Burhoe 1957, 3).

Its detailed argument shows that "A Step Toward a Scientific Theology" foretells the programmatic thrust of Burhoe's vision. As noted above, his proposal for the conference was implied in his "stage" theory of the evolution of human knowledge of values, and the argument against relativism became an important part of his later writings that justified the relevance of science for religion and the study of values. That argument also contained the core for the later development of his theory of the role of religion in biocultural evolution. Although religious faith and the sense of ultimacy seem rooted in animal faith and trust in instinctual strategies for survival, ritual and myth are rooted in prehuman behavioral strategies for survival that, at the human level, become codified in cultural traditions. Inasmuch as religions are the bearers of the ultimate values and cultural strategies for human survival, religion is the essential core of culture—its moral and motivational center. A scientific theology that shares the concern of neoorthodoxy for the wisdom of religious traditions, but reforms that wisdom in the light of contemporary science, was envisaged as a way to salvation in an age of science. This new approach would therefore be scientific in method, seeking to establish conceptual theological entities in a way similar to the way in which conceptual physical entities are established. Examples of reinterpretation were given, such as original sin and the notion of faith in ultimacy. Finally, hope for a worldwide religious reformation was expressed on the basis of scientific consensus across sociocultural boundaries. It must be stressed, however, that it was not Burhoe's perception that science will *replace* religion, but rather that a scientific approach to religion and morals will further the evolution of religious expression by integrating traditional religious wisdom with the knowledge of the sciences, producing a scientific theology.

SCIENCE—A POTENTIAL BASIS FOR A WORLDWIDE RELIGIOUS CONSENSUS

At the end of December 1957 Burhoe drafted another proposal, this time for the 1958 Star Island conference, on the theme ''Science—a potential common denominator for the world's religious factions or—Towards a universal belief about hope and morality for man through science.'' His proposal built upon a theme of the 1957 conference, that a scientific approach could provide a way to unite the different religions of the world through concurrence on the nature of reality. Also, his proposal returned to the primary aim of the Coming Great Church conferences: to lift discussions among leaders of different faiths above their boundaries of creed or dogma into the realm of common understanding. The Star Island conference was therefore proposed along the lines of a scientific study of the religious function in human culture (Burhoe 1958).

As a guide for all participants, ten common characteristics of religious faiths were proposed:

(1) a program of human salvation;
(2) which provides the individual believer with personal hope
(3) in the face of catastrophe from the natural environment,
(4) in the face of catastrophe from the inequities of human society, and
(5) which orients the individual to a moral or socially cooperative program;
(6) and which grounds these hopes and orientations in a logic following from special beliefs
(7) about the ultimate nature of man
(8) and about the ultimate reality or powers of the universe in which he lives,
(9) which beliefs describe man and the universe in ways that usually differ drastically from the native or common-sense views,
(10) for the purpose of making sense and harmony out of what otherwise might appear as an unreasonable and hopeless condition of man (Burhoe 1958).

Two suppositions were emphasized: (1) ''kinship between beliefs about the facts of *human* values and beliefs about the facts of *mechanical* or *material* values,'' and (2) an evolved religious tradition is useful in its cultural setting and is not likely to be abandoned as a result of scientific knowledge.

There is respect for each religious tradition. However, this does not mean that we should expect no changes in beliefs and practices, but, insofar as any beliefs can be shown to have been primarily responsible for the basic behavioral characteristics of any viable society, it would seem that we should have to recognize their essential validity regardless of how poorly they might stand in an alien logic.

Burhoe defined *religion* as "the historical evolution of those beliefs and practices characteristic of men in contemplating the extreme conditions and ultimate goals of life." "The conference," Burhoe wrote,

hopes to move forward from an analysis of the functions and methods, which are more or less common to all religions as thus defined, to an attempt to reformulate these functions and methods in the light of the new vision of reality provided by the sciences. . . .

This appeals to us as a likely avenue to religious and moral belief capable of binding all men under a common and proper respect for the powers that be and an optimum development of the potentialities of human beings.

This effort further presupposes that it is not likely that man will be able to achieve a reasonably peaceful and creative society in an age of science without a specific and articulate formulation of the religious problems in a new way. . . . Man has eaten from the tree of knowledge, and he has thereby become responsible to nourish his ideals and ultimate goals as well as his more immediate bodily needs by the fruits of this tree. Not only by the sweat of his brow shall he gain life, but it seems clear that he is required to gain better knowledge or understanding of the source and potentialities of his own being, and that is what we mean by religious understanding. (Burhoe 1958, 3–4).

Members of the Advisory Board, however, were not ready to analyze historical religions; they doubted, moreover, that a liberal scholar, partisan to the Marxist and Communist faith or even to any traditional religious faith, could be found to review religions with scientific objectivity. They seemed to favor a methodological treatment of the issues raised in Burhoe's proposal: "Mr. Phillips [suggested] that we ought to approach directly, without a review of all the historical variations, the question of the purpose or function of religion for today. . . . Mr. Harrington [suggested] that we ought to work at practical problems that concern the clergy here and now" (IRAS 1958a). It was therefore agreed that the conference "seek to clarify the function or purpose of religion in the light of modern science."

JOINT SEMINAR WITH THE ACADEMY ON THE FUNCTIONS OF RELIGION

Jointly, on 12 April 1958, the Academy and IRAS sponsored a seminar on the functions of religion in the light of modern science at the House of the Academy. The seminar, according to the syllabus drawn up by Burhoe, was "not to defend any existing religion, but to examine the functions of religion . . . in an attempt to define some hard core of agreement about its function in a scientific culture." Accordingly, the first session dealt with the question "What functions which properly may be called religious are also vital to a scientific culture?" Because the syllabus also directed the seminar toward defining a religious function common to every human society, the central definition to be examined was: "The function of religion is to interpret to man his ultimate concerns in relation to the totality of powers, known and unknown, with which he must come to terms."

The second session proposed "to illuminate the problem of the effective operation of religion in a scientific culture" by answering several questions: "What are the characteristics of a scientific culture? What do the traditional religions offer in terms of ultimate concerns or values which is viable and effective in such a culture? What limitations on traditional religion are placed by a scientific culture?" The third session dealt with the question "What novel or scientific contributions are conceivable to enhance the religious functions in a scientific culture?" (IRAS 1958b).

These and similar questions pertaining to the "Contributions of Science to the Role of Religion" were also pursued at the next Star Island conference (18–25 August 1958).

In spite of the agreement on the IRAS program of the previous year (1957), differences about the direction of the Institute arose during the Star Island meetings of the Advisory Board, especially over the visitation of theological seminaries (for which the Danforth Foundation had promised a grant of $3,000). "[Ian] Barbour suggested that we involve local people. . . . Montagu, Kemble, and Bradshaw wondered if we did not need to put our own house in order before talking with theological faculties; we really don't know where we stand and we don't have much commonly accepted material to present" (IRAS 1958d). Inasmuch as the discussions resurrected "the problem of our purposes," a committee (Rutledge, Barbour, Bradshaw, Burhoe, and Hoagland) was asked to report the next day on "our purposes," and it reaffirmed the goals or purposes set forth in the IRAS constitution.

Burhoe and Montagu recommended the September 1956 proposal for such a program and, as well, a committee of scholars to devise a program of studies for the restatement of religion in the light of science so as to make the former more effective in the modern world. The consensus was that such a program was too ambitious, and some members urged maintenance, instead, of an "open forum for exchange of ideas between professional people in religion and science rather than to present conclusions." Among other topics, discussion of the next summer conference queried the effectiveness of having such a group. "Mr. Montagu and others had been pointing out the fact that the discussions among . . . advanced scholars . . . were frustrated by answering and talking to . . . so many people whose understanding of the problems is obviously of a different level. . . . On the other hand, it has always been urged by some of the Board that the mixture is advisable" (IRAS 1958d).

It was also recommended, this time to the Council, "that the time has arrived for election of members of the Institute who are not necessarily members of the Advisory Board." Thus there was another divergence between those who wanted to pursue a more exclusively academic route, to develop a body of commonly accepted doctrine, and those who thought it best to be more inclusive, emphasizing an "open forum" for the exchange of ideas.

BURHOE'S ASSESSMENT OF IRAS AND FUTURE DIRECTIONS

The Institute again held monthly meetings in Boston during the 1958–59 academic year. In spite of reservations, the Council in November authorized Burhoe to draft an announcement of the Danforth-funded visitation program and send it to theological schools. President Booth thereupon scheduled a discussion of the goals and methods of IRAS for the January meeting: "IRAS arose, he [Booth] said, in response to a felt need of coordinating the religions and the science of our time as the basis for a more effective social ethics. Sufficient years have passed that the work accomplished can be reviewed and decisions reached as to whether the Institute should survive and, if so, in what directions it should move." After Lyman Rutledge and Edwin Kemble were asked to lead the discussions, the meeting reported that resignations had been received from Ashley Montagu and B. F. Skinner, both of whom had been members since 1955.

Rutledge asked Burhoe for a statement from his perspective as "Program Builder" for IRAS, and Burhoe responded with a lengthy assessment of IRAS at the meeting on Sunday, 18 January 1959. Like a prophet, Burhoe espoused his vision of IRAS as a reformation movement in an age of science. He acknowledged what others had said, that he was closer to the common core of IRAS than most, but he made it clear that he was more a servant than a "program builder." "I think the program has been built by God rather than by me, if I may say so." He then reviewed events leading to the forming of IRAS, his personal history, and the severance of religion from the "insults" of modern knowledge in Barthian neoorthodoxy, which he saw as justified under the assumption that science was being used to destroy human life. Because he had "an automatic and enthusiastic appreciation of the power and beauty of rational systems for building ever more valid and useful pictures of reality," he was convinced that science could play a positive role in religion (Burhoe 1959). "In my view we do not have much time. Human destiny is being overwhelmed by a chaos of morals and of personal faith or hope that in the context of the technological products of science threatens to extinguish life on earth. And I do not believe the schizophrenic retreats to more primitive forms of religion can be a true solution. Only a religion that stands on its feet in the light of science can save man for the future. It is the formation of such a religion which I conceive to be the task of IRAS" (Burhoe 1959).

It is difficult to assess how such a prophecy was received. That it did *not* bring the membership closer to agreement on the purposes of the Institute is indicated in a letter from Burhoe to the IRAS Council at the end of January 1959. The letter was his resignation as editor and chairman of the publication committee (consisting of Carl Bihldorf, Walter Clark, Sophia Fahs, and Edwin Kemble), which had been appointed the previous summer. Suggesting that the publication program be reformulated or be abandoned for the time being, Burhoe cited "a lack of a truly common notion of and enthusiasm for a publication program," combined with his limited time "for pursuing a clarification of differences" among members of the committee, as reasons for delay in publishing the first issue (Burhoe 1959).

It is clear that Burhoe did not feel he had persuaded enough persons to engage in the publication program he envisioned for IRAS. After deliberation in August 1959, the Council abandoned publication of a journal, dismissed the committee (with thanks), and gave the go-ahead to publish a book of papers. Under the editorship of Harlow Shapley, *Science Ponders Religion* appeared in the fall of 1960 (Shapley 1960). Subsequently, IRAS published a pamphlet of a talk by A. F. C. Wallace (Wallace 1961) and another volume of papers, edited by Edwin Booth, under the title *Religion Ponders Science* (Booth 1964). A journal of the kind Burhoe envisioned had to wait for more support, until 1966, when *Zygon: Journal of Religion and Science* was established in cooperation with Meadville/Lombard Theological School in Chicago.

MISSION TO THEOLOGICAL SCHOOLS

One aspect of the IRAS program, which eventually led to an advanced studies center and a scholarly journal of the kind envisioned by Burhoe, was its mission to theological schools. From 1956 on, the IRAS Advisory Board had envisioned arranging conferences of IRAS scientists and theologians on the faculties of theological schools. A $3,000 grant from the Danforth Foundation provided impetus, and successful approaches were made to several theological schools. Conferences were held at Boston University School of Theology (1957 and 1959), Chautauqua Institution (1957), Hartford Seminary (1957 and 1959), Wesley Seminary (1959), the Theological School of St. Lawrence University (1959), Colgate-Rochester Divinity School (1960), Alfred University Theological School (1960), and Crane Theological School of Tufts University (1960).

In 1960 Malcolm Sutherland, who had been a Unitarian minister in the Boston area and vice president of the American Unitarian Association, became president of Meadville Theological School in Chicago. Sutherland was acquainted with the work of IRAS and, in particular, its program of sending teams of scientists and theologians to theological schools to interest them in the potential of the sciences for theology. Shortly after his arrival in Chicago, he contacted Burhoe and IRAS to help him to test out his hope that some of the implications of the sciences for religion might become a significant element in theological education. The result was a Colloquy between Religion and Science "to provide disciplined discourse between religion and the sciences in order that the liberal ministry may reflect appreciation of the implications of those insights that illumine the nature of existence and the condition of man and to suggest [a] possible response," as the 1963–64 Meadville catalogue put it. Burhoe contributed three lectures to the first series of colloquies on 3–4 April 1961 (Burhoe 1961). In his first lecture he argued, on the basis of his interpretation of the cosmic, evolutionary picture of the modern sciences, that theology is "queen of the sciences": "As the science which by definition informs men of their highest and most ultimate goals or concerns, theology is by definition forever queen of the sciences." The second lecture, "Fall of the Queen," on problems contributing to the decline of theology centered on its reluctance, or inability, to integrate its doctrines with the new knowledge developed by the sciences. The third lecture, "The Restoration of the Queen," argued that a new theology will be integrated with the sciences. The colloquies continued for three years and included seminars led by Alfred E. Emerson, Sanborn Brown, Ralph W. Gerard, Henry Nelson Wieman, James R. Killian, and Edwin P. Booth.

By 1961 the IRAS mission to theological schools seemed to have "paid off" rather well, and there was a good prospect of a firmer connection with the theological community. Burhoe's connection with this community was the realization of a dream he'd had from the time he went to Andover-Newton (in 1932) to express a credible credo of religious faith in an age of science. Three years later, in 1964, he was asked to join the theological faculty at Meadville in an experiment to do just that.

BURHOE'S VISION: "SALVATION IN THE TWENTIETH CENTURY"

The first expression of Burhoe's conceptual system was his essay "Salvation in the Twentieth Century," written in the winter of 1957 and revised for publication in 1960 in *Science Ponders Religion,* edited by Harlow Shapley. The essay is significant not only because it is the first published account of Burhoe's vision of a scientific theology, but because it indicates that his thought had taken an all-but-final shape as early as 1959.

The essay, programmatic in character, presents his assessment of the human condition as it was then, to which his proposal of an integration of religion and science was addressed, and outlines his evolutionary theory of religion and its implications for theological formulation and religious revitalization in light of the sciences. The following analysis of the essay will therefore give a general picture of Burhoe's vision for theological reform and revitalization of religion in the light of the sciences as it was articulated by 1959.

The essay's very title poses the question: From what does humanity need to be saved in the twentieth century? Burhoe's answer is that the emergence and development of scientific methods of knowing and the successful use of scientific knowledge in developing technologies have radically altered the conditions for human life. His assessment of the human situation is that science has so drastically altered the conditions for human survival that traditional means for organizing and perpetuating human life are no longer adequate. However, he does not propose the replacement of traditional programs for human salvation; rather, he proposes the extension and reformation of traditional religion in the light of the sciences—that is, a "scientific religion":

And yet I wish to suggest that our salvation today lies in religion. This suggestion is preposterous enough; but, when I add that religion must also be scientific, both the high priests of the traditional religions and the high priests of science will surely say that this is a mad prophet indeed, for he puts words together that everyone knows cannot be put together—a scientific religion! (Burhoe 1960).

In the first part of the essay, Burhoe substantiates his assessment and his belief that a scientific religion is the way to salvation. In brief, his argument is that culture is a continuation and extension of biological evolution, and religion has evolved as the integrating core of culture. Human cultures, he argues, evolve in response to their environments, and science, which is a way of acquiring and accumulating knowledge, and is also a product of this evolutionary process, has temporarily destabilized culture by producing a new environment of ideas and cultural technologies. The integration provided by traditional religions is a prescientific cultural adaptation, with the consequence that if a religion does not adapt to the environment by integrating the sciences with its traditions, the central, integrating core of the culture will dissipate. The result will most likely be the extinction of such a culture, which on a global scale means extinction of the human species. For religion to continue its integrating function for human culture, it must be integrated with the sciences.

In the second part of his essay Burhoe presents his program for integrating religion and science, exemplified in the work of IRAS. This integration must begin with imaginative attempts to reformulate religious doctrine in terms of the scientific rendering of reality. "The sciences," Burhoe said, "are the most powerful handmaidens theology has ever had" (Burhoe 1960, 77). Thus a scientific religion begins with development of a scientific theology:

The sciences are building a more honest, more effective, [richer] picture of the hidden secrets of our own natures and of the vast reality in which we live and move and have our being than has ever before been built.

Science provides the basis for a new testament, a new scripture of truth about man and his destiny. Even if this revelation should gainsay any of the previous revelations of human destiny, it will be believed anyway. . . .

But it has been the discovery of several of us that the revelations of the sciences do not basically gainsay traditional religious doctrines; science does not so much destroy as it fulfills the previous testaments. . . .

Thus the scientific approach to religion will be a humble effort to read the true story of man, his relation to the source of his being, and his consequent duties and privileges. This approach will respect the existing religious traditions in the same way that agricultural sciences respect agricultural traditions. The scientific approach to religion, like all former valid approaches, cannot possibly transgress the sovereign law of the source of being, but can only seek to discover or reveal it (Burhoe 1960, 77–78).

The goal that he has in mind is "a full system of doctrine satisfactory to both the scientifically established picture and to basic religious needs" (Burhoe 1960, 85).

Burhoe gives "in rough outline some of the major doctrines which I believe will be established and become effective in giving man a proper sense of direction and hope in the age of science.'' On doctrines of revelation and truth, he says:

The newly developed scientific epistemology is of greatest significance for our views of religious knowledge. . . . Religious doctrine formulated in the light of science . . . will grow and change as the sciences do. . . . In science man has found the way to build the most reliable and convincing doctrines. . . .

Concerning the doctrine of creation, he writes:

The creation of man . . . is the product of a long and complex development under what are presumed to be essentially universal and invariant laws of operation. . . . The infinity in which we live and move is in reality one, not many. . . . The scientific faith that all things are variants in a single system, that one law rules the cosmos from end to end . . . is so high that we have little doubt that there is a continuity from man to amoeba to molecule. There is no separation of man from his origin nor from his fellow men. We are indeed all brothers and all children of the same father. . . .

Concerning the relationship of God and man:

In view of the scientifically painted picture of the vastness and pervasiveness of the source and ground of our being, and in view of its orderly design and the immutable law according to which it operates, the only sensible conclusion for man is to recognize it as his ''lord and master,'' and to spend all his days in discovering and applying what it indicates he must do if he is to have life and more abundant life. . . . Man can most properly conceive of himself as a local agent and servant of the creative process of the universe. Man is privileged through his continued searching to know ever more of its design and to participate in ever larger measure in the development of its program. . . . In truth man must identify his own meaning . . . in terms of the program of this ultimate reality. . . . Every being and event is an inseparable part of the sacred whole. . . . Each man is inextricably bound up in the web of a great whole. . . .

And finally he writes concerning the doctrines of soul and immortality:

Man's kinship with his Creator [is the basis of] man's kinship with all his fellow men, a kinship that is deeper than blood. . . . To serve my fellow beings and to serve the program of evolving life is to serve my own deepest and most significant self. This is my ''true,'' my ''spiritual'' being, or my ''soul.'' . . . [The body] must be recognized realistically for what it is, a transient and small portion of the invisible soul or whole which it is created to serve. This core of soul of my being, the sciences reveal, is older than the hills, a growth of hundreds of millions of years, still conserved as living values in my genotype. Another aspect of my enduring soul . . . is revealed in the impossibility of separating me from the cultural types or forms, which take me back thousands of years. . . . To serve this deeper self is not to discount the body or other structures of the more immediate present, for all this is a part of my being. All life is sacred. . . . More than that, all things in the cosmos are sacred, whether we call them living or not. It is this interpretation of the scientifically revealed world as sacred, including my own nature, which I think we need to recognize if we are to get away from our idiotic schizophrenia that spirit and values lie in one world, and matter and knowledge lie separately and independently in another (Burhoe 1960, 84–85).

Burhoe concludes his essay with "Call for Apostles for the New or Scientific Reformation":

The main point of this paper is simply to suggest and very roughly outline my interpretation of why some of us think a sound and effective religious doctrine now can be established in the full light of modern science (and probably cannot be without that light). Many seem to feel that the further advance of human civilization, or perhaps even the continuation of life on this planet, urgently requires such a doctrinal system to provide the grounds for a more dynamic and effective morality and morale among enlightened men. We call upon all who can see the problem and who have the background and imagination to join our mission in exploring and developing this new insight into the necessities and opportunities provided to us by that reality in which we live, and move, and have our being (Burhoe 1960, 85–86).

CONCLUSION

This discussion of Burhoe's vision and its role in the development of IRAS should manifest Burhoe's conviction that a scientific approach to religion is the most hopeful rationale for contemporary religious inquiry. His faith in a scientifically sound and morally effective system of religious doctrine was shared, to a greater or lesser degree, by many of the scientists and religious scholars associated with IRAS. Burhoe was an interpreter of the religious and theological implications of the ideas generated and explored by this group, as well as by others associated with the Academy, and it was to this community, as it expanded over the years, that Burhoe sought to relate his developing scientific theology. Whenever he spoke about the roots of his scientific approach to religion and theology, he traced it to the beginning of his association with this community, in 1947, and it was from this community that Burhoe continued to receive new ideas and concepts with which he expanded and refined his basic argument. This accounts for the fact that Burhoe developed a scientific theology in terms of highly generalized concepts and ideas, for a scientific approach entails the search for those highly generalized conceptions in terms of which specific instances can be interpreted and explained.

The promise of such an approach for developing sound and effective religious doctrine with the resources of the scientific community prompted Unitarians acquainted with IRAS to utilize its resources. Burhoe also became the chief formulator and organizer of this approach as it was developed in IRAS activities. As a result, two parts of the IRAS program were realized: a center for advanced studies and a scholarly journal for religion and science.

The next chapter will discuss these latter developments and the further formulation of Burhoe's scientific theology within the context of the Unitarian Church.

REFERENCES

Booth, Edwin Prince, ed. 1964. *Religion Ponders Science*. New York: Appleton-Century-Crofts.

Brown, Sanborn C. 1963. *Institute on Religion in an Age of Science: A Ten-Year View, 1953–1963*. Boston: IRAS.

Burhoe, Ralph W. 1955. "Religion in an Age of Science." *Science* 122 (30 December): 1277–78.

———. 1956a. "Proposal for Development of Program." Distributed to the Advisory Board and Council of IRAS, 14 September. Mimeo.

———. 1956b. "Religion in an Age of Science." *Science* 124 (12 October): 690.

———. 1957. "A Step toward a Scientific Theology: Notes on Certain Aspects of the 1957 Conference on Religion in an Age of Science." Report distributed to the IRAS Advisory Board, December. Mimeo.

———. 1958. "Draft Proposal for the 1958 Conference on Religion in an Age of Science," 1 January.

———. 1959. Letter to the Council of IRAS. Undated, probably written around 31 January.

———. 1960. "Salvation in the Twentieth Century." In *Science Ponders Religion*, edited by Harlow Shapley, 65–86. New York: Appleton-Century-Crofts.

———. 1961. "Theology, the Queen of the Sciences"; "The Fall of the Queen"; "The Restoration of the Queen." Papers delivered to initiate the Colloquies on Religion and Science at Meadville Theological School, 3–4 April.

———. 1967. "Five Steps in the Evolution of Man's Knowledge of Good and Evil." *Zygon* 2 (March): 77–95.

IRAS. 1956a. Report on discussions of 24 and 25 January.

———. 1956b. Constitution draft of April, approved 5 May with corrections noted.

———. 1956c. Program for the 1956 Summer Conference on Religion in an Age of Science.

———. 1956d. Advisory Board meeting records. 16 August, 2 October, 16 November.

———. 1957a. Program for the 1957 Summer Conference on Religion in an Age of Science.

———. 1957b. Council meeting records. 31 July.

———. 1958a. Advisory Board meeting records. 12 January.

———. 1958b. "What Are the Functions of Religion in the Light of Modern Science?" Announcement of a seminar jointly sponsored by IRAS and the American Academy of Arts and Sciences. Mimeo.

———. 1958c. Program for the 1958 Summer Conference on Religion in an Age of Science.

———. 1958d. Advisory Board meeting records. 19–24 August.

———. 1958e. Council meeting records. 20 September.

———. 1958f. Council meeting records. 16 November.

Margenau, Henry. 1950. *The Nature of Physical Reality: A Philosophy of Modern Physics.* New York: McGraw-Hill.

Northrup, F.S.C. 1947. *The Logic of the Sciences and Humanities.* New York: Macmillan.

Shapley, Harlow, ed. 1960. *Science Ponders Religion.* New York: Appleton-Century-Crofts.

Wallace, Anthony F.C. 1961. "Religious Revitalization: A Function of Religion in Human History and Evolution." IRAS pamphlet.

III Developing the Vision among the Unitarians, 1954-1964

Burhoe's vision, as outlined in the previous installment, influenced a number of Unitarian leaders, who were associated with the Institute and concerned to deepen the theological dimensions of their denomination. The purposes of IRAS and the kind and quality of its activities stimulated them to try a similar approach (Greeley 1971). In two related activities, Burhoe played a significant role, and he involved persons connected with IRAS. In 1959, six commissions on The Free Church in a Changing World were given the task of assessing the shape of liberal religion in the Unitarian and Universalist churches and stimulating thought about what might be regarded as the common message and mission of the new Unitarian Universalist Association. And in 1960 a theology and science emphasis was developed in the educational program of Meadville Theological School in Chicago. Burhoe's two related activities contributed to the establishment of a research and teaching center, and of *Zygon: Journal of Religion and Science,* within Meadville, a denominational theological school.

Thus the 1956 IRAS "Proposal for Program" was on its way to being realized, although not in the form that IRAS leaders would have anticipated. The establishment of a center and a journal far outside the Boston area and in connection with a denominational theological school was far from the thinking of most of the scientists and scholars associated with the American Academy. Reflecting on his Academy years, Burhoe later wrote, "For various reasons, the Academy Committee [on Science and Values] could not work directly with religious institutions, and many in the Academy wondered why one should bother with dying institutions" (Burhoe 1967, 17). In fact, he reflected, "My friends in the Academy . . . urged me to stay [in Boston, with the Academy] to the point that I had to bias weight on the other side of the argument to go into a religious institution." (Burhoe 1967, 18). Because Burhoe's primary concern was revitalizing religion, developments in the Unitarian church seemed most promising (Burhoe 1967, 17). Also, they gave him the opportunity to articulate his vision more fully in relation to the liberal religious tradition.

Many within the liberal tradition feared that any effort to articulate a theological consensus would compromise the basic principle of religious freedom. Conversely, Burhoe and some other Unitarian leaders believed that the identity and health of the liberal churches seemed at great risk without some articulation of basic beliefs and doctrines. Accordingly, in his work with the Commission on Theology and the Frontiers of Learning he developed his vision for a bold reformation of religion in the light of the sciences. This vision implied the necessity of doctrine, the possibility of doctrinal consensus without sacrifice of freedom, and the revitalization of traditional religious wisdom integrated with contemporary scientific knowledge. One significant outcome was a recommendation to establish a research center along the lines of Burhoe's vision. Burhoe's involvement with such developments within Unitarianism shows his concern to develop theology in the context of modern science so as to effect the revitalization of religion in contemporary culture.

THEOLOGY AND THE FRONTIERS OF LEARNING

Burhoe was an active member of the Arlington Street Church, where Dana McLean Greeley was pastor. Greeley knew of Burhoe's involvement with the Academy's Committee on Science and Values, and he wanted to make a connection between that group and liberal church leaders, particularly those in the Coming Great Church conferences on Star Island. In 1952 he invited Burhoe to make such a connection. The outcome was the 1954 conjunction of these groups and the formation of IRAS. Greeley, a charter member of IRAS, served on its council. In IRAS and in Burhoe's vision for revitalizing religion, Greeley saw potential for the development of a program in the Unitarian churches. Then in 1958, Greeley was elected president of the American Unitarian Association (AUA), and consultations with Burhoe were part of a process that led to a proposal for a department on Religion and Science and the Frontiers of Learning in 1959.[1] In this period, plans were being made to merge the AUA and the Universalist Church of America into a new Unitarian Universalist Association. This thrust, in turn, expanded into six commissions to assess the religious climate in the new denomination.

The six study commissions on "The Free Church in a Changing World" were approved on 21 September 1960. Burhoe was appointed secretary of Commission II, on "Theology and the Frontiers of Learning," and named as one of its nonclergy members. His commission presented a preliminary report to the delegates of the organizing meeting of the Unitarian Universalist Association in Boston, 11–13 May 1961. Together with Robert Tapp, the chair of the commission, Burhoe wrote and edited the final report, which was published and presented to the UUA General Assembly in Chicago in May 1963 (Unitarian Universalist Association 1963).

The preliminary report set forth the task of Commission II, on Theology and the Frontiers of Learning:

The function of this Commission is to review and clarify the basic assumptions or beliefs found within the denomination, to intensify the confrontation of our religious faith with new knowledge in the various fields of learning, and to facilitate constructive thinking towards a creative religious philosophy and convictions for our time (Unitarian Universalist Association 1961).

There was fear in some quarters that the commission would attempt to write a new creed for the denomination. This fear was also addressed in Robert Tapp's report on Commission II:

Our Commission plans to strengthen . . . those who take seriously the need for continuous critical thinking in religion. Within the free church there cannot be, and should not be, theological conformity. There may well emerge a consensus, however, if we come together seriously enough and long enough. Such a consensus is already evident within the freedom of scientific inquiry. Our conviction is that vital religion is not so different from science but that a similar community may grow here (Unitarian Universalist Association 1961, 10).

The report went on to state that "liberal religion thrives on the frontiers of learning and sees the sciences not as a threat, or even a challenge, but as an exciting source of wisdom for our lives and our dreams" (Unitarian Universalist Association 1961, 11). In spite of the fear of creeds as indicative of theological conformity, the hope of a theological consensus drawing on the resources of the sciences indicates the influence of Burhoe's vision in the work of the commission.

The prevalence of an anticreedal reaction to the work of the commissions was symptomatic of a key problem facing the denomination. Paul Carnes, in his "Commentary" on the final reports of the commissions, observed that "the presence of the fear indicates that we need a more thorough awareness of our Universalist and Unitarian traditions" (Unitarian Universalist Association 1963, 162).

Perhaps in some quarters the free churches' respect for the reason of individuals and freedom or toleration for differences of religious belief had become uncritically dogmatized into suspicion of any attempt to give positive expression to that which constitutes the faith of religious liberals. It was this problem that the commissions were formed to address, so that some beginning might be made to stimulate the expression of a shared religious stance.

This background helps make clear a number of factors influencing Burhoe's writings. First, he had to fight an uphill battle to affirm the desirability of a religious doctrine based on common features of personal or religious belief. Second, he had to show that the development of such doctrine would not compromise freedom of belief. Third, he had to promote the idea of rationality of belief. Fourth, he had to fight distrust of traditional religious doctrines. The fears he addressed are deeply rooted in the liberal tradition. The free church historically has attracted those who found traditional Christian orthodoxy—Catholic or Protestant—repressive. Therefore, attempts to state any principles of belief were highly suspect, because it was feared that this would only lead to a new orthodoxy. If this were imposed on the basis of some authority, it would abrogate all personal and religious freedom.

"SOME THOUGHTS ON THE FUTURE OF LIBERAL RELIGION" (1962)

The reaction within the denomination against a consensus on religious doctrine stimulated Burhoe to address the problem. He saw this resistance as a fundamental obstacle to revitalizing religion. Therefore, if there were to be an integration of religion and science, it would have to be worked out conceptually, accommodating the full range of religious and scientific scholarship. In 1962, in his article "Some Thoughts on the Future of Liberal Religion," he stated that the future of religion depends on a "well-developed, coherent and . . . homogeneous structure of religious beliefs and doctrines" (Burhoe 1962a, 16). Characteristically, Burhoe was not concerned to offer specific doctrines; rather, he tried to motivate the denomination to accept the serious challenge of developing such a structure with the aid of the sciences.

Burhoe appealed to the idea that world problems might be resolved without recourse to war if some worldwide religious consensus could be achieved on the basis of freedom and reason.

The key doctrines of liberal religion may be said to be the essential foundation stones for building a peaceful world society: the doctrine of freedom (respect for the personalities and convictions of other men), the doctrine of the use of reason rather than authoritarian decree to establish common values, and the doctrine of the quest of the not-yet-achieved broad and encompassing religion that binds all men in brotherhood (Burhoe 1962a, 12).

He argued that the strengths of liberal religion are also its weaknesses. Because its proponents commonly believe that freedom and rationality are incompatible with doctrinal agreement, they leave matters of belief to the individual. Tolerance of a wide variety of religious beliefs implies, however, that no particular beliefs or doctrines are important.

This makes one wonder whether liberals, in their fear of arbitrarily imposed "final truths," have come by an opposite route to the same conclusion that seems prevalent among the neo-orthodox as a result of their fear of the "truths" of science: that man's reason is impotent to deal with questions of religious belief (Burhoe 1962a, 14).

Burhoe proposed that the way in which scientific doctrine is developed can serve as a model for liberal religion. Scientific doctrine is not a matter of individual opinion but a system of coherent doctrine, built up out of pieces validated by complex and universally accepted procedures. Scientific doctrine does not violate the sanctity of the conscience, for "the ultimate arbiter is usually said to be what any individual can observe to happen or to be" (Burhoe 1962a, 20). And it need not be feared as authoritarian, for it is always undergoing revision. Burhoe argued further that if liberal religion built its religious doctrines "with the tested bricks of scientific doctrine," it could produce "a doctrine which will be the basis for a moral and spiritual conviction necessary for creative world community in an age of science" (Burhoe 1962a, 22).

Burhoe's vision spoke directly to the doctrinal impasse of the UUA. This, no doubt, was the reason denominational leaders sought his consultation and leadership. Drawn into this environment, Burhoe was given an opportunity to develop his vision, for it provided a possible approach by which Unitarians and Universalists could express the content of their faith in an age of science. Indeed, Burhoe's contributions were concerned with demonstrating that a scientific approach to religion would produce a bona fide theological understanding that would not compromise the liberal doctrine of freedom.

GOD AND THE WORLD: LEARNING THE COSMIC LAW OF LIFE

The commission also met periodically to discuss papers of its members, and Burhoe presented one of three major papers at such a meeting on 25–26 September 1961. The theme to be addressed was "The Concepts of *Theos* and *Kosmos,* the Stage of the Human Drama," and Burhoe's paper, "Religion and the Kosmos of 20th-

Century Science," developed his vision around the relation of God and the world. It argued for the need to formulate a theology that was well integrated with contemporary cosmology. The first part of the paper developed the God-world relationship, using the image of the cosmic law of life. By selecting this guiding image, Burhoe showed his kinship with the tradition of natural theology. In particular, this image represents an idea similar to, if not the same as, the Stoic conception of the logos, especially the *logos spermatikos*.[2] Burhoe then explored the idea that the evolution of life can be viewed as learning the requirements of the law of life and passing acquired knowledge of it to subsequent generations. He then developed the idea that religions can be viewed as cultural systems in which knowledge of the law of life for human survival is acquired and transmitted. In the final section, he argued that human culture is in a precarious position because the religious information necessary for life has not sufficiently incorporated the new requirements and understandings that have been illuminated by the sciences; hence, the integration of scientific knowledge into religious doctrine is immediately essential for the continued survival of human culture.

Of particular note is the fact that Burhoe placed at the beginning of his paper a quote from a paper that the anthropologist Anthony F.C. Wallace had just presented at the 1961 IRAS Star Island Conference. Evidently, Burhoe did not have the time to work Wallace's idea into the body of his paper, but he saw in it support for his ideas on the function of religion:

But religion does not offer just any solution: it characteristically offers a solution which assures the believer that life and organization will win, that death and disorganization will lose, in their struggle to become the characteristic condition of self and [of the meaning of the] cosmos. And religion further attempts to elucidate and describe the organization of self and [of the meaning of the] cosmos. Religion then may be said to be a process of maximizing the quantity of organization in the matrix of perceived human experience. Religion maximizes it, perhaps, beyond what rational use of the data of this experience would justify, but it thereby satisfies a primary drive. We must, I think, postulate an organization "instinct": an "instinct" to increase the organization of cognitive perception. Religion and science, from this point of view, would seem to be the more direct expressions of this organizational instinct (Burhoe 1961a, 38–39).

Wallace's observation that humans are programmed with a drive to organize their world of experience supports Burhoe's basic argument, for he wants to show that this drive is rooted in the very nature of the cosmos as the drive toward life and more abundant life.

Burhoe began his paper with a brief argument to suggest the identity of the concepts of theos and cosmos:

But if the total phenomena of the universe are considered to have a common hidden source, then the terms 'god,' 'spirit,' or 'theos' may be said to denote this one, common, universal source of the cosmos. And if, as in a dominant philosophy of modern science, the hidden sources, or causes of phenomena are taken along with the phenomena themselves to be inseparable from the nature of the world, then it becomes difficult to separate the denotation of 'theos' from that of 'kosmos' (Burhoe 1961a, 1).

Burhoe's concept of God, characterized by a radical immanence, functions heuristically as a means for elaborating the God-world relationship in terms of contemporary cosmology.

Contemporary science postulates that the cosmos is an "ordered, harmonious, seamless fabric," and the laws by which humans describe its structures and operations are presumed to be universal, potentially unified or integrated, and inseparable from the events that reveal them. This postulate, which has encouraged conceptual integration among the separate sciences in this century, underlies the development of evolutionary theory, which understands the human to be an event in a continuous process of selection of viable patterns of existence.

A page or two later, Burhoe says:

It should be noted that the concept of "selection" is central for cosmic and local evolution. Selection is a concept that says the environment or kosmos determines what will be allowed. . . . It sounds awfully like the Hebrew Psalmist's statement that man should seek the law of God, for those who abide by it will prosper and those who flout it will surely perish. . . . The "selector" in [contemporary] cosmography is firmly believed to be inseparable from the nature of the lawful phenomena of the total cosmos. . . . Hence one can conclude that individual and social human life will flourish or perish according to whether men operate in accord with what these laws and conditions say will be permitted or not be permitted as patterns of life. . . .

However, man does not know much about the laws of the cosmos and their requirements for his potential development. . . . As a finite creature he has been endowed by his creator, the cosmos, according to contemporary cosmographers, with the potentiality to grow in favor with his creator indefinitely to the extent that he serves that creator—that is, to the extent that he succeeds in discovering and living in accordance with the requirements presented by that creator and cosmos. In fact, the more man incorporates this law (cf. the religious doctrine of divine incarnation) the more he becomes identified with it, and becomes a co-creator in the events of the universe. But the moment he turns his back on the law of the cosmos, then he loses his life. This, I think, is a fair statement of the implications of the beliefs commonly held by contemporary cosmographers in the various sciences (Burhoe 1961a, 3-4).

This section extends a concept of law, embedded deep within the Judeo-Christian tradition, to include a cosmic evolutionary sense. Doing what is required by the law maintains a covenant relationship with God, for both the individual and the community. From this perspective, adhering to the law is intimately connected with learning the law, that is, gaining knowledge of the requirements. It was to this task that Burhoe turned his attention.

In the next section, "Learning the Cosmic Law of Life," Burhoe developed the idea of the evolution of knowledge from his conference proposal, "On the Nature of Truth" (Burhoe 1957, 1). Citing Ralph Gerard's idea that the "fixation of experience underlies evolution, it underlies development, and it underlies learning," Burhoe gave a definition of learning that draws upon the evolutionary process of trial and error. "Learning is a name for the many different mechanisms of irreversible changes which produce progressive development, the underlying dimension of all becoming" (Burhoe 1961a, 5a). Viable patterns are determined by the cosmic law of life: "Certain patterns are bound to arise, even if only on a probabilistic basis; and once arisen are bound to persist and to enter in the determining of future patterns of events" (Burhoe 1961a, 5). From the smallest particles to the complex human organism, all entities are involved in countless trials of relatedness. "Each time they hit upon a viable pattern, it was automatically stamped with approval by the selector, the cosmic reality, and the new pattern of structure and behavior persisted, and continues in living species, including man, until this day" (Burhoe 1961a, 4). The learning of viable patterns is cumulative, and with the appearance of self-reproducing complex molecules we have the beginning of life. The self-duplicating DNA molecules had accumulated the knowledge of a long series of trials and errors and "had 'learned' to form complex patterns that could persist and evolve by new adaptations" (Burhoe 1961a, 5). The DNA molecules became the vehicles for genetic learning, the accomplishments of which were faithfully transmitted from generation to generation.

With the evolution of complex central nervous systems, a new and faster method of learning was made possible for the organism. This method is different from genetic learning in that its products can no longer be transmitted in the genetic code from one generation to the next. With the arrival of the human animal, "a still newer method of learning came into bloom which allowed the learning of the individual through his central nervous system to be transmitted to future generations"—namely, cultural transmission or cultural inheritance, whose main organ is language (Burhoe 1961a, 5a). Three subsequent emergents are mentioned: "The symbolic system of the language, which had grown for thousands of years by a kind of unconscious selection for its efficiency and value, was found to be able to produce new wisdom simply by means of its own operations [reason and logic]." Science added to reason and logic "the test, the proof, the observations, the experimentally contrived observation." A by-product of the sciences is the computer—an "auxiliary extension of the brain." Burhoe then concluded this description of the evolution of the learning of the cosmic law of life: "With all these marvelous new creations in the human capacity to learn and know the law of the cosmos, man stands at the threshold of a [new] kind of life" (Burhoe 1961a, 6).

Introducing a discussion of "The Function of Religion in Relation to the Cosmic Law of Life," Burhoe pointed to the conservative element in the evolution of learning. "While natural selection built in the capacity of the genes to mutate, change, discover, or learn, it nevertheless definitely limited this capacity." The process of sexual recombination, which emerged as a mechanism for controlled or limited mutation, permits the recombination of the already tested and viable genotypes in the gene pool of a species into countless variations of the genotype that thereby have a high probability of viability. "When a pattern of 'know-how' for life has been achieved and fixed, and when changes (mutations or learning) do not provide a more viable outcome, then selection establishes the viable pattern without change." In science, one finds tremendous conservative forces that insist on the faithful transmission of the body of the scientific tradition before a new scientist "is allowed to create new variants, to do creative research, on his own. . . . The same kind of conservative forces are found in all social institutions which succeed in promoting a successful form of life." These conservative forces serve as a limit on variability in order to ensure the continued viability of a species or society. "The living system is the high value that learning and knowledge must serve" (Burhoe 1961a, 7). Humans in the several subcultures of learning must not "forget that their only viable function is to serve the life of the society of which they are a part, and if their neglect is the source of crumbling of their society or civilization, then they pass away with it" (Burhoe 1961a, 8).

In this context, Burhoe introduced his interpretation of religion. "The function of religion in culture . . . is primarily one of transmitting or communicating the most essential or sacred accumulations of the 'know-how' of life" (Burhoe 1961a, 11). Religions are part of the evolutionary process, and doctrines, cosmologies, and beliefs change and develop within a religion. Natural selection seems to operate on religions as well as species, for anthropological studies "have noted that when a religion becomes non-viable the society that adheres to it becomes non-viable." By analogy, Burhoe emphasized that religions are a central control for a viable pattern of cultural life.

"One might say by way of figure of speech that the religions are to human culture what the central nervous system is to an organism and what the critical genes are to the genotype of a species" (Burhoe 1961a, 9).

Human culture was in a precarious position because the applications of greater knowledge on the frontiers of human learning are changing the conditions for a viable human society. Because the traditional institutions have become obsolete in their language and failed to relate to the imagery of contemporary cosmology, they are unable to convincingly communicate their wisdom so that it motivates behavior. Burhoe criticized the liberal tradition for its failure to meet the current crisis. While many liberals assent to the validity of the contemporary imagery of the cosmos, they eschew doctrine, cosmic theory, or theology as having relevance for the "good life." But we can no more rely on primitive religious conceptions than we can on primitive technologies. "And still less can we rely on the inborn animal instincts for love and goodness, which were wonderfully adequate for their time" (Burhoe 1961a, 10).

Burhoe concludes with a prophecy and a challenge to liberal religion:

On these grounds I prophesy that to the extent that a religious institution fails to integrate its system of religious beliefs, its theology (its doctrine of theos), with the contemporary doctrines of cosmos, it will wither and pass away; and that a religious institution which successfully formulates a doctrine concerning the central human values of the present era out of the actual pieces of the new cosmology as it is coming from the frontiers of learning, this institution will serve mankind and will prosper with the more successful or viable kinds of men it produces (Burhoe 1961a, 10).

The challenge for liberal religion was to formulate the most sacred doctrines of life for an age of science. Such a formulation would then relate religious problems of life to contemporary cosmology and integrate traditional religious insights into a new theology, expressed in the system of symbols of that cosmology. The new theology needs to be credibly expressed so as to motivate humans to make their pattern of living more viable. "This credibility of doctrine is a gift awaiting the religion that successfully formulates a theology well integrated with the prevailing cosmology. . . . This is the great need of the world and the greatest responsibility and opportunity of liberal religion" (Burhoe 1961a, 13).

CRITICISM OF BURHOE'S PAPER BY THE COMMISSION

The discussions at the meeting of the commission focused on certain critical issues in the implications of Burhoe's paper and some disagreements about the role of science in theology and religion (Burhoe 1961b). Two aspects of the discussion are highlighted here, the first of which deals with theological problems in Burhoe's emphasis on the concept of cosmic law and his response to them. Some of the theologians did not see how Burhoe's position could encompass such traditional religious concepts as love, justice, freedom, and a God who cares. Burhoe replied that the law of natural selection implies that God cares about the cosmos and humanity. However, in order to arrive at this implication, that which is essential must be identified with the lasting structures of evolution revealed by the sciences. "If in our concept of man we identify ourselves with the temporary and transient and in the long-run erroneous phenomena, we are certain to conclude that the cosmos does not care for us" (Burhoe 1961b, 7). He maintained that religious thinkers for millennia had developed concepts of soul and spirit to signify these lasting structures, but that contemporary religions do not recognize the same notion in current scientific developments.

Burhoe was asked in which of two streams of Christian theism he stood: "God cares if (1) you stand in a relation of right belief and know God's name, or (2) you stand morally in terms of obeying his laws?" He replied that doing the will of God or the law comes first, because the law of the cosmos is written into the heart of man, into his genotype. However, with respect to human culture, which extends the cosmic law of life by means of symbolic systems, right belief or knowledge of God is essential.

One scientist objected to Burhoe's putting God into the description of the laws of life, to which he responded "that the conditions the cosmos sets for life, however revealed, is equivalent to God." His thesis, he said, was not contrary to the description of the sciences. "The purpose in using the term 'god' is to connect the languages of religion and science" (Burhoe 1961b, 8). When theologians queried him on the absence of the concept of forgiveness, Burhoe intimated that the notion of forgiveness needed to be thought anew, from an evolutionary perspective, in which the individual body does not have much of enduring value, but its enduring value is dependent on the role the individual plays in the evolving cosmos.

In sum, this discussion pointed to the problem of a caring God in Burhoe's thought. However, Burhoe's response indicates that, for him, the idea that "God cares for me" cannot be separated from God's caring about the whole cosmos, and must be interpreted in that light.

As for the second aspect, Burhoe attempted to persuade the commission, and through it the denomination, of the necessity to formulate doctrine in the light of contemporary science. (Burhoe subsequently developed this concern in a number of articles in denominational publications.) The discussion centered around the issue of whether theological development could be enhanced by the procedures of science, as Burhoe proposed. A number of persons expressed doubt that religious problems could be resolved by a rational or intellectual approach, because religion is primarily concerned with problems of meaning. Burhoe responded that if the intellectual statement of the human predicament does not have value, there was no point in a Commission on Theology and the Frontiers of Learning. "We ought to make up our minds as a Commission whether we are willing to risk the hypothesis that one can formulate theoretical statements about basic values in life so that the statements will motivate ethical behavior and internal wholeness" (Burhoe 1961b, 3). He said that if the commission could not accept the idea that we can advance to a better life by a theological formulation grounded in the sciences, it had no further business to conduct. "Liberals today boast of adherence to reason, but fail to apply it to problems in religion."

Discussion of Alfred Stiernotte's paper, "On the Idea of Theos," raised the question whether religious experiences, especially of the cosmos, require expression in metaphor or myth, rather than rational discourse, since in religious experience we participate in a tremendous mystery. Burhoe pointed out that scientific theory is a kind of myth and that scientific myths are better than older myths because, with them, we can speak more reliably about things that have the greatest meaning for us, including religious experience. "We [owe] a great debt to traditional religious interpretations of the cosmos, but we do not have an interpretation that works for the modern world. This is an opportunity for liberal religious institutions to develop such an interpretation or theology that works under today's sophistication" (Burhoe 1961b, 5).

On 9 March 1962 Burhoe read a paper, "The Evolution of Science and Religion," at the Public Forum Series in the St. Louis Unitarian Church (Burhoe 1962b). The structure of the paper was similar to that of his "Religion and the Kosmos of 20th-Century Science" (summarized above); however, he did not use the image of learning the cosmic law of life, suggesting that the discussions in the commission meetings had made some impact. The aim of the paper was to illuminate a "vision of the opportunity for the great new religious awakening in the light of science" and to kindle "some small flame of resolution to work for the advancement of this 'spiritual' reformation, this new kingdom of heaven" (Burhoe 1962b, 17). The first part developed the idea of evolution as the acquisition of the knowledge of good and evil. "This will be a scientific account of human genesis," Burhoe said, "and a review of what the sciences tell us about the sources of our knowledge of those religious values that we call good and evil" (Burhoe 1962b, 1). Sacred or religious knowledge is accumulated in and transmitted by two evolving systems of information, or "languages." The first is information encoded in the genetic material—"And the code inscribed in these chemical molecules is more sacred, more faithfully followed, than any of the religious and moral laws of the past few thousand years" (Burhoe 1962b, 2).

The second system is the information encoded in human languages. With the evolution of the human brain, a new and faster kind of evolution was possible. "The new power of man for advancing and enriching life lies in large measure in his ability to inherit knowledge of good and evil through his culture, primarily through what we call language" (Burhoe 1962b, 4). He introduced the term *idenes* to refer to this culturally evolved and transmitted knowledge— "cultural genes." Scientific development of idenes has greatly increased the rapidity of learning knowledge of good and evil. However, the rapid increase of scientific knowledge has radically altered the culture and threatens disintegration, unless this knowledge is integrated with religion. With this argument, Burhoe arrived at the heart of his message: to spell out "a great opportunity for religion."

(1) The attainment of religious beliefs and teachings that are as sound and credible as those of the sciences; (2) a consequent deepening religious motivation for moral behavior and the attaining of a sounder basis for religious feelings of purpose, hope, and love from the scientific information underlying human values, goals, and motivation; (3) the development of a religion which can capture the minds and hearts of the whole population, not only of the United States, but of the whole world, because it will be inseparable from the universal appeal and credibility of scientific knowledge generally; (4) the re-establishment of a true integration of religious and secular knowledge, wherein theology will again become the Queen of the Sciences. (Burhoe 1962b, 13).

To grasp this opportunity "will require the participation of large numbers of us to develop institutions to more effective forms by applying scientific knowledge to them" (Burhoe 1962b, 14). He appealed to the hope of a world community, based on scientific knowledge.

Burhoe attempted to persuade Unitarians to seize the great opportunity for religion—a religion integrated with the sciences—and his vision was persuasive enough, and sufficiently held in common among members of the commission, to make its way into the final report.

In an environment that was highly suspicious of, if not hostile to, any form of religious orthodoxy, and at the same time receptive to modern scientific thought, it was only natural that Burhoe emphasized the scientific worldview and the methodology of the sciences as the basis for a religious formulation. Moreover, it provided the basis for developing doctrines that would preserve individual freedom and rationality. Such doctrines would not become dogmatized but would continually develop in the light of growing knowledge of God's world and all the requirements for life. Such doctrines, furthermore, would hold the promise for a worldwide religious consensus as a basis for a world community. However, because of the pluralistic character of Unitarians and Universalists, Burhoe's ideas have had only a limited appeal among some of them.

FINAL REPORT OF THE COMMISSION

When the commissions on the Free Church in the Changing World finished their work in 1963, the final report of Commission II (Theology and the Frontiers of Learning) addressed the theological problems facing the denomination in two parts. The first part of its report, largely written by Robert Tapp, described the theological diversity within the denomination and the "liberal style" of its members. The second part, largely written by Burhoe, called for theological reconstruction in the light of the present-day frontiers of learning. After the report concluded with specific recommendations, the final draft was edited by Burhoe and, like all committee reports, submitted to the members of the commission for their approval.

In sorting out the unity and diversity within the denomination, the first part of the report acknowledged the historical roots of Unitarianism and Universalism:

> Unitarianism originated as an emphasis upon the unity of God, the humanity of Jesus, and the dignity of man, as well as upon the full use of reason in religion. Universalism was born of the concept of a God of love, and universal salvation as over against a partial atonement or the salvation of a few or the elect. Both bodies . . . are now united in our new Association for a "free and disciplined search for truth as the foundation of our religious fellowship."
>
> It has been our ideal always to be hospitable to dissent, as the path to a new knowledge. As we have striven to maintain the spirit of unity, a creative diversity has woven many strands of thought into the fabric of our faith (Burhoe and Tapp 1963, 24–25).

The report then identified six major theological emphases in the "Liberal Perspective," which is characterized by an openness to theological diversity. These six emphases, it was pointed out, do not exist in pure form but "occasionally are interfused in individuals and usually coexist in our groups": Christian liberalism, Deism, mystical religion, religious humanism, naturalistic theism, and existentialism. Four common experiences, identified as the "Liberal's Style," described the denomination's unity in diversity: this-worldly concerns, ethical responsibility, commitment to democracy, and community/religious bases.

The report went on to state that the commission held that "thought should have primacy over feeling" and that "major human problems ought to be solved in terms of both the perspective and style of religious liberalism and in terms of the best available truths from the frontiers of learning" (Burhoe and Tapp 1963, 30). An included minority report said that some members of the commission held that personal religious experiences should hold primacy over theological interpretation.

The second part of the report was written by Burhoe, and in spite of the fact that the commission reviewed and made changes in it, Burhoe's vision shines through. This section can be viewed as an argument for a new, natural theology to solve the credibility crises stemming from new knowledge and ideas from the frontiers of learning. Its structure closely follows Burhoe's "Religion and the Kosmos of 20th-Century Science" as it reexamines the religious concept of revelation to show "our conviction that the frontiers of learning are relevant to more adequate theological constructions." However, revelation is treated as the source of knowledge, which is defined as "acquired or learned information that orients or guides . . . behavior." A "fresh view" of the "natural history of 'revelation' " is given on the basis of insights from contemporary sciences and scholarship (Burhoe and Tapp 1963, 35).

Biological sources of revelation are pointed out in the genetic code, the learning capacity of the evolved brain and central nervous system, and the capacity for language in the evolved and developed human brain. Religious revelation is interpreted as an imaginative problem-solving experience, induced by frustration and tension. In the human, a new kind of evolution becomes dominant: "Culture is made possible by the powers of the human brain to construct and manipulate images of the world . . . The evolution of the cultural patterns has now become a major process of human evolution."

In the context of human cultural evolution, revelation means "a source of truth incorporated in a cultural tradition" (Burhoe and Tapp 1963, 37). The environment's selection of novel patterns "builds into cultural patterns, such as languages, boats, or religions, a beautiful 'wisdom' and order" of which humans are "still largely ignorant and unconscious" (Burhoe and Tapp 1963, 38). Religions evolved as a cultural agency to transmit "from person to person the central patterns for the ordering of life." As religions evolved, there emerged what we now call theology. Explanations of the major concerns of life were given in terms of a network of environmental powers that determined human destiny, commonly called *gods,* and "the religions cultivated the proper attitudes and ways of living and dealing with them."

This "natural history" of revelation is completed by a discussion of "two more recent emergents in the evolution of 'revelation' in human culture": reason and modern science. Reason resulted from the discovery that "the wisdom of the logic unconsciously built into . . . language could be used consciously as a tool" for learning. Modern science is not merely a collection of facts. "It is the conceptual structure or theories that constitute the scientific revelation" (Burhoe and Tapp 1963, 39). Science is characterized by its testing of new theories and its openness to sincere and competent critics.

Some believe that there is now a religious crisis because religion is not rooted in modern scientific knowledge and has therefore lost its persuasive power and meaning. The challenge for the liberal churches is this: "Can we generate a dynamic religious belief which fits with and draws its strength rationally from the present frontiers of learning?" The assumption that science cannot deal with values was also challenged: "The whole point of this review of the evolution of 'revelation' has been to make clear that modern science is but the most recent in a long series of instruments for the revelation of knowledge of values for human living" (Burhoe and Tapp 1963, 41). The report then took up two questions concerning problems facing the denomination: "Is theology a good word for liberals?" and "Does science inhibit religious feeling and understanding?" Thus it was argued that a scientifically grounded system of doctrine about the highest human values was needed to give a new meaning and motivation in the present age. "Its power to evoke positive emotions of religious joy is only slightly developed, because we are standing at the very beginning of a period of serious reconsideration of natural theology" (Burhoe and Tapp 1963, 43).

A paragraph that was not in the final report but was stapled into Burhoe's copy is worth quoting for it shows the central relationship between science and religion in his vision.

When scientifically acquired information becomes relevant for resolving problems of high concern, of how man may best relate himself to whatever is most significant for sustaining his being, then the results should yield the experience of religious salvation just as the results of scientific notions may yield the experience of salvation from toothache. . . . [3]

Two claims must be stressed. First, the application of scientific information to religious problems can result in better, if not richer, religious experiences. Second, humans, with the use of scientific concepts, can become more conscious, intentional, and hence more effective in dealing with problems resulting in pain and anguish. That is to say, humans may become more effective, because better informed, in their healing of individuals or achieving social justice—healing the pain and anguish produced by injurious social policies.

The report concluded with "factors favoring a new theology":

In the first place, the use of scientific notions in theology is in keeping with our liberal traditions of rationality, of open-mindedness, of freedom of belief and conscience. Because of its tradition, the UUA should lead in developing religious potentials of the sciences.

In the second place, the crisis of the 20th century offers an opportunity for growth and for service in this area, unparalleled for new break-throughs in the evolution of religion and human culture. This crisis is a resource for the growth and usefulness of a religious association.

In the third place, the scientific approach to religious doctrine offers a new potentiality for achieving consensus in religious thinking. . . . The traditional liberal tolerance and respect for differing beliefs will be guaranteed by a scientific approach to theology. . . . Religious unity without coercion, without dogmatism, should be the natural by-product of a scientific approach to theology. (Burhoe and Tapp 1963, 44-45).

Five recommendations followed: "(1) Preserve denominational breadth. (2) Intensify our dialogue with ecumenical Christianity. (3) Intensify the dialogue among the historic religions. (4) Develop an institute for advanced study of theology in relation to the frontiers of learning. (5) Enrich the frontier-content of denominational curricula." The most significant of these recommendations, at least for the purposes of this study, was (4), development of an institute for advanced study. Combined with other factors, this recommendation led to establishment of such an institute at Meadville Theological School in Chicago, with Burhoe as its director.

The point of this discussion of Burhoe's involvement with the Commission on Theology and the Frontiers of Learning has been to show (1) that Burhoe had a bold vision for the renewal of liberal religion wherever it existed; (2) that this vision informed the denomination through the work of the commission; and (3) that the theological climate of the denomination formed the context in which Burhoe continued to develop his vision. Burhoe was sought out because he offered entrée to scientists concerned with human values and religious issues, as well as for his visionary leadership in the development of the Institute on Religion in an Age of Science. He was recognized as a person with a religious and theological vision of value to the denomination—that approaching religion in a manner similar to that of the sciences could produce a consensus on doctrines for human life with such universal validity as to be the basis for a worldwide religious consensus.

BURHOE AND THE NEW DESIGN AT MEADVILLE

Various factors and events, not the least of which was the recommendation of the Commission on Theology and the Frontiers of Learning, resulted in a theology and science component in the program of Meadville Theological School. Upon dissolution of the group known as the Federated Theological Faculty at the University of Chicago Divinity School in 1960, Malcolm Sutherland was called to succeed Sidney Mead as president. Thus the new situation presented the challenge to design a new curriculum for Unitarian Universalist theological education to replace the curriculum under the Federated faculty. Convinced of the positive relation of the sciences to theology by his background in psychiatric social work, Sutherland had become acquainted with the work of IRAS in the summer of 1959, when he was vice president of the AUA, and President Dana Greeley suggested that Sutherland accompany him to the 1959 IRAS Star Island summer conference for a one-day meeting on denominational matters. Sutherland was impressed with the work of IRAS, and the summer of 1960 marked the beginning of his long association with the Institute. (He served as vice president from 1963 to 1967, as president from 1967 to 1968, and on 31 July 1980 he was elected an honorary vice president.) When Sutherland assumed the duties of president at Meadville, he looked for ways of enticing Burhoe to Meadville to lead in the development of a program for integrating theology and the sciences into the education of Unitarian Universalist ministers (Sutherland 1986). He first sought Burhoe's assistance in starting a regular colloquy on religion and science, for which Burhoe gave the opening set of seminars.

In a study of the five Unitarian and Universalist theological schools in 1962, Harold Taylor recognized the Meadville colloquies on religion and science as one effort to meet the need for liberal ministerial students to explore the issues and implications of the sciences for religious and philosophical speculation. He noted, however, that the need would not be properly met until science became a regular part of the curriculum (Unitarian Universalist Association 1963, 63). What became known as "The Taylor Report" was the outcome of a study of theological education commissioned in 1959 by the American Unitarian Association, largely in response to the need of

financial support for the theological schools at the time of denominational consolidation (Greeley 1971b, 143–46).[4]

From the perspective of this study, one important criticism per-
vades the report: Unitarian Universalist education was too dependent on traditional Protestant theological models and thus not in
keeping with the spirit of liberalism. The curricular pattern of
required courses, centered in the traditional Protestant theological
disciplines, needed to be reoriented to the understanding and task
of ministry in the liberal tradition, yet expanded to include an understanding and appreciation of other religions, the intellectual geog-
raphy of contemporary culture, the creative and performing arts, and
the contemporary sciences.

One year later, in May of 1963, the six study commissions on the
Free Church in a Changing World issued their final reports.
Although the work of the Commission on Theology and the Frontiers
of Learning did not have a great impact, it stimulated development
of a research center as part of a new design for theological education
at Meadville.[5]

The New Design of Theological Education was announced in the
spring of 1964, as follows:

Meadville's revised curriculum seeks to bring theological inquiry into a
disciplined and demanding engagement—first, with contemporary knowledge
about the nature of man and his environment and second, with contemporary
life as it is in its being lived.

There is a tremendous body of radically new knowledge about man and the
source of his being that has not yet been seriously related to man's religious
quest and his search for supreme values. In this new knowledge is much to
illuminate and substantiate some of the basic insights of ancient religious
traditions and at the same time there is much that would reform and provide
radically advanced insights needed for the new levels of human life possible in
a civilization transformed by science and technology (Meadville Theological
School 1964, 5).

In addition to the traditional focus on the religious traditions of
Western culture, two departments formed the substance of the New
Design: the departments of (1) Theology and the Frontiers of
Learning and (2) Theology and the Church in Society. The former
was established "for the purpose of relating theology or religious
theory to the insights, conceptions and models of reality of contemporary knowledge at its most advanced levels" (Meadville Theological School 1964, 7). In connection with this department, a Center
for Advanced Theological Studies was also announced; it was to
conduct a program of research and study, guide advanced-degree
scholars, engage in a publication program, and conduct programs
of continuing education.

BURHOE'S CONTRIBUTION TO NEW DESIGN

Burhoe was instrumental in shaping the theology and science component of the New Design because, in the fall of 1963, Sutherland had asked him to draft a prospectus for a center for religion and science at Meadville. Burhoe relates this request in his own words:

Whatever may be the mood and need of a secular generation which cannot believe in the traditional representations of God who established the duties and guaranteed the spiritual values of men, one straw in the wind, showing incipient interest on the part of the religious and theological community in the relatively quiet recent growth of interest among scientists in problems of sacred human values, blew into my face in the fall of 1963. Sitting in my office in the House of the American Academy of Arts and Sciences in Boston, I received a phone call from Malcolm Sutherland, President of the Meadville Theological School, affiliated with the University of Chicago. He had been contemplating his experiences at some of the summer conferences of the Institute on Religion in an Age of Science in which I had played a part. There we had for a decade been bringing some [of] the nation's greatest scientists to speak about what they thought their science had to say about religion and human values. Sutherland had been impressed with our notion that the sciences might be revelatory for man's religious concerns, and asked if I would help him find a scientist to head up a new department at Meadville to try to relate the new knowledge about man and the source of his being to man's religious quest (Burhoe 1966, 1).

Burhoe's response was a twenty-page draft on 21 October, titled "Center for the Integration of Religion and Science. Meadville Theological School. A Prospectus" (Burhoe 1963b, 12b). In an accompanying letter, Burhoe recommended Julian Huxley, then seventy-six years old and about to retire from his position with UNESCO, as "the best man in the world . . . competent to deal with this field" (Burhoe 1963a).

The rationale for the center was, in essence, a statement of Burhoe's vision of a program for the integration of religion and science. The argument for the need of a program to integrate religion and science was first clearly stated in "Salvation in the 20th Century" (discussed in chapter 2 of this biography). It was further developed in Burhoe's work on the Commission on Theology and the Frontiers of Learning. In the prospectus, this argument was developed to become the rationale for the center at Meadville.

The Center for the Integration of Religion and Science was to be "set up after the fashion of contemporary research and development centers" to implement "a program to revise theological doctrine in a scientific fashion," using the "full application of contemporary scientific methods and theories to ascertaining truth concerning religious problems" (Burhoe 1963b, 6–8). The scientific approach would assure convergence and coherence of doctrine, thereby resulting in commitment to an evolving "free consensus" on doctrine that had been verified in fact or experience. "Some of our exploration suggests that a scientific evolutionary perspective will facilitate our seeing hitherto unrecognized or unanalyzed wisdom in all religions," Burhoe had written in the prospectus. The theologian and religious scholar would have an important role to play: "It is only with the religious scholar's and theologian's understanding of the religious arts that new inventions from the sciences can be adapted and instituted effectively to improve the religion of the future." The rationale concluded with the following statement:

We are convinced by an already existing but limited investigation of religion in the light of the sciences that religion is essential for a viable society, that great wisdom inheres in its traditions even when they have not been translated into a modern idiom. We are further convinced that new translations, revisions, and additions can yield an ever-widening consensus on theological doctrines which are as true, and effective for their purposes, as those in the medical and other professions which have already integrated their arts and doctrines with those of the sciences. (Burhoe 1963b, 9)

Two important personnel needs were identified. Because the policy would be "to relate religious theory honestly and seriously to the mainstream of contemporary science," advisory board members and consultants would be selected "from among the very highest leaders" in the sciences and philosophy.

The curriculum and research of the center "will always be oriented to religious and theological questions, the sciences being involved only to the extent that they may shed useful light for the understanding of these problems." Burhoe identified five areas of research (revelation, man, God, salvation, and church) and criteria for the application of scientific knowledge.

Many different areas of science have changed our illumination of parts of these questions. . . . But a sheer increase in knowledge does not mean it is immediately applicable. . . . In each profession the knowledge has to be selected and further tailored to fit its own special problems. . . . In theology the doctrines must be formulated in such a way as to be effective in the ministrations of the churches suitably to orient men's motivations and emotions to personal and social (or moral) well-being and good behavior. . . . Certain avenues of pragmatic or empirical tests will be constantly applied to the teaching as well as the related research, such as tests of the depth of conviction and the consensus which the hypotheses develop in those involved, as well as of the degree to which the hypotheses can be justified in the relevant existing scientific body of doctrine. (Burhoe 1963b, 13–14)

The program of the center would develop a curriculum of courses, periodic seminars and colloquiums, research projects, a bibliography and library, special conferences and study groups, testing of practical applications in the churches, and a journal for international communication in the integration of religion and science. The prospectus ended with a sketch of five courses in each of the identified research areas, to which Burhoe prefaced the remark, "These may be called a religious exegesis of the scriptures of the contemporary sciences."

BURHOE IS OFFERED, AND ACCEPTS, THE LEADERSHIP OF THE THEOLOGY AND SCIENCE PROGRAM AT MEADVILLE

Sutherland and some of the Meadville/Lombard board saw the potential of such a program for revitalizing liberal religion, so Burhoe was invited to give a series of lectures (in January 1964) as part of the Religion and Science Colloquy series. This was also to be the occasion for exploring the possibility of his joining the Meadville/Lombard faculty to direct the new program in theology and science.

In three lectures on the metaphysics of physics, Burhoe sought to show what revelations physics may have "for building a rational theology that could provide a validity of authority and power for the clergyman that equivalent applications of the sciences provide for other professions, such as medicine" (Burhoe 1964a, B30a). These lectures presented the way in which Burhoe intended to continue developing his theological position.

Sutherland, who finally persuaded Burhoe to take the leadership of the theology and science program at Meadville, described the occasion:

I remember the wonderful combination of enthusiasm and caution with which he responded to my inquiry and invitation. I realized that as the Executive Officer of the American Academy, he was settled for life if he wished to be and I wonder now at my own audacity to ask him to leave that for so insecure an experiment, uproot himself from his beloved New England and come to Hyde Park. As I developed my invitation I could see him internally beginning to fashion concrete possibilities, but outwardly he was cautious. (Sutherland 1987, 21)

The offer to direct the development of the Meadville program put Burhoe in a difficult situation. However, he was committed to the project, to which he had already given substantial work and direction. In a letter to Sutherland he wrote:

In my opinion, the proposed Meadville expedition is the first realistic one for conveying a group from the shores of the Judeo-Christian tradition to the new world of theological illumination and religious conviction by the light of the sciences. . . . I associate myself wholeheartedly with the mechanism for dealing with this harvesting of new crops of knowledge for theology and religion which you have outlined . . . in your Proposals for Curriculum Revision. . . . I have to confess that I am somewhat torn up inside by conflicting opportunities and loyalties. . . . I await word from you with much interest on what you and your board finally propose. Then I may have some difficult confrontations and decisions. (Burhoe 1964b)

Within a few weeks he was offered the position of professor and director. Besides his regular duties, then guiding the theology and science component of the New Design, Burhoe faced the difficult decision to leave his "beloved New England" for the Hyde Park neighbourhood of Chicago. It meant giving up his lifelong attachments in the Boston area, uprooting his family, and resigning his position with the American Academy of Arts and Sciences. The Academy, a hub of mental and cultural activity, provided with Burhoe a broad and deep acquaintance with all the men and women working on intellectual frontiers. This rich interdisciplinary milieu was the context in which Burhoe had developed his vision for the integration of religion and science. Now he faced separation from those who shared his concern for formulating human values adequate to meet the challenges of the cultural crisis, especially those in the Academy Committee on Science and Values, many of whom had formed the nucleus of IRAS. Many of these friends saw no reason to bother with religious institutions and urged him to stay with the Academy (Burhoe 1967, 17–18). What then motivated him to leave Boston and his secure and rewarding position with the Academy?

An answer to the question, in Burhoe's own words, is found in his "Review and Farewell" to the American Academy of Arts and Sciences of 13 May 1964:

I explained my resignation to the Council nearly three months ago, but I think I owe an explanation to all of you. At Meadville Theological School I have been invited to continue the exploration of the basic postulate of my formative years which is also a postulate which has played a role in this Academy's renaissance—an integration of science and human values. In a sense, for the past seventeen years you have been preparing me for this task. But, at Chicago I expect to be freed of administrative duties and to find more time to gather the threads I have been spinning with my left hand for three or four decades and to weave them into a more ordered pattern of teaching and writing. Many of you have urged me to write this book, and now I am taking you seriously. I could not take it seriously and continue to render the service you need in an administrative office here.

I can state the main theme of my future work in the words of the 1946 report of the Commission on the Present Status and Future of the Academy: ". . . the spirit, purpose, and essential logical and instrumental methodology of science can be applied more or less readily and successfully to any and every form and aspect of human knowledge." I would emphasize that this includes our knowledge of basic human values, values which traditionally have been called ethical and religious.

Two thoughts console me as I leave this bright port of warm friends. One is that I am sailing with the same model of the world and the same compass and charts of the heavens with which you have provided me, and I go in search of one of the same treasures you have been seeking. The second is that a number of you with whom for years I have been dreaming of reaching this shore of better moral and spiritual insights and motivations by means of scientific understanding will in some degree continue to sail with me. I trust that we are not really separating even though some of my routines will be changed. (Burhoe 1964c, 11–12)

The opportunity to work full-time in developing his postulate that an integration of science and religion is essential for human welfare overshadowed other considerations.

Burhoe's work with the Academy had provided an intimate acquaintance with persons working on the frontiers of research, and discussion with these persons had provided the resources with which he had articulated his program for reforming religion. Although a number of members were concerned to apply scientific methodology to the study of basic human values, the focus of the Academy was not on Burhoe's religious and theological concerns. These he had developed in his spare time, apart from—but sometimes through— his work in IRAS and with the Commission on Theology and the Frontiers of Learning. His intention to devote himself to theology, which he had given up in the 1930s under economic pressure, could now be realized in the position offered by Meadville. In addition, it seemed as if the unrealized expansion of the IRAS program could be achieved at Meadville—namely, an integral component in theological education, a publication program, and a research center.

The work of the Institute [IRAS] led . . . to my accepting the invitation of President Malcolm R. Sutherland and the Trustees of Meadville/Lombard Theological School affiliated with the University of Chicago, to head what may have been the first theological-school-sponsored department ever commissioned to research, develop, and teach theology using the modern sciences as a prime resource. (Burhoe 1981, 16)

NOTES

1. The "Suggested Agenda" in a "Prospectus for Commissions," approved on September 21, 1960, noted: "as far as it is possible, the costs of these Commissions may be taken from the item in the Development Fund package for Religion and Science and the Frontiers of Learning, and the Commissions themselves will thus serve as a substitute for that proposed department."

2. For the Stoics, Logos was the principle of all rationality in the universe, and as such it was identified with God and with the source of all activity . . . In man it was the power of reason in his soul, 'resident' in him and also, when spoken, it became 'uttered' reason. For the Stoics the principle of morality was 'living in accordance with nature,' and as the nature of man was to be rational and indeed nature as a whole was the rational product of Logos, living according to nature could be equated with living according to Logos. Logos was thus the source of law and morality." (*Encyclopedia of Philosophy* 1967).

3. Typewritten note stapled into Burhoe's personal copy of *The Free Church in a Changing World*. It appears to be an alternative formulation of the last paragraph on page 43 of *The Free Church*.

4. The committee commissioned Harold Taylor, retired president of Sarah Lawrence College and philosopher of education, to conduct an independent, in-depth study of the five schools where the majority of Unitarian Universalist ministers were trained: the Theological School of St. Lawrence University, the Harvard Divinity School, the Meadville Theological School, Starr King School for the Ministry, and Crane School of Religion at Tufts University. Because Taylor's study comprised the bulk of the final report (pp. 23–133), it came to be known as "The Taylor Report." This study came on the heels of the Survey of Theological Education in the United States and Canada, sponsored by the American Association of Theological Schools and undertaken in 1954.

5. Dana Greeley, in a paper on the occasion of Meadville/Lombard Theological School's 125th anniversary, reflected on the work of the six commissions: "I was extremely pleased with their findings, but those findings never adequately caught the attention of local churches and the denomination. We neither gave the findings a proper forum nor assimilated what they had to say to us" (Greeley 1971a, 23). Issues of social justice seem to have overshadowed consideration of the reports of the six commissions at the Chicago General Assembly in May 1963. (See Greeley 1971b, 105–6.) Greeley also notes the direct connection between IRAS, Commission II, and Meadville: "From the latter [IRAS] were born both a denominational commission of the Unitarian Universalist Association and finally a department of the Meadville Theological School of Chicago" (Greeley 1971b, 200).

REFERENCES

Burhoe, Ralph Wendell. 1957. "On the Nature of Truth." Proposal for the 1957 Conference on Religion in an Age of Science. January. Burhoe papers. Chicago. Mimeo.

———. 1961a. "Religion and the Kosmos of 20th-Century Science." Paper presented at the meeting of the Commission on Theology and the Frontiers of Learning of the Unitarian Universalist Churches, 25–26 September. Burhoe papers. Chicago. Mimeo. This paper quotes from an unpublished manuscript by Anthony F.C. Wallace, "Religious Revitalization: A Function of Religion in Human History and Evolution." This quotation also appears in Wallace, Anthony F.C., *Religion: An Anthropological View.* (New York: Random House, 1966), pp. 38–39.

———. 1961b. "Third General Meeting, 25–26 September 1961. Summary for the Record, by Secretary Burhoe." Burhoe papers. Chicago. Mimeo.

———. 1962a. "Some Thoughts on the Future of Liberal Religion." *Crane Review* 5 (Fall): 12–23.

———. 1962b. "The Evolution of Science and Religion." Paper presented in the Public Forum Series at the St. Louis Unitarian Church, 9 March. Burhoe papers. Chicago. Typescript.

———. 1963a. Letter to Malcolm Sutherland. 21 October. Burhoe papers. Chicago.

———. 1963b. "Center for the Integration of Religion and Science, Meadville Theological School: A Prospectus. " 21 October. Burhoe papers. Chicago.

———. 1964a. "The Lord of Mankind" in two parts: "Source and Sustainer of Man" and "Image of God or Soul." Burhoe papers. Chicago.

———. 1964b. Letter to Malcolm Sutherland. 18 January. Burhoe papers, Chicago.

———. 1964c. "A Review and Farewell." Communication presented to the Academy of Arts and Sciences at its 184th Annual Meeting, 13 May.

———. 1966. "The Campus and the Creator." *Faculty Forum* 37 (May): 1–2.

———. 1967. "Science and World Religious Consensus." Paper for the Meadville Colloquy, 20 April. Burhoe papers. Chicago.

———. 1970. "Commentary on J. Bronowski's New Concepts in the Evolution of Complexity." *Zygon* 5 (June): 98–101.

———. 1972. "Natural Selection and God." *Zygon* 7 (March): 20–63. Also appears as chapter 4 in Burhoe 1981.

————. 1981. *Toward a Scientific Theology*. Dublin: Christian Journals.

Burhoe, Ralph Wendell, and Robert Tapp. 1963. "Theology and the Frontiers of Learning." In *The Free Church in a Changing World*, ed. Ralph Wendell Burhoe and Robert Tapp, chapter 2. Boston: Unitarian Universalist Association.

Encyclopedia of Philosophy. 1967. S.v. "Logos," by G. B. Kerferd.

Greeley, Dana McLean. 1971a. "The Unitarian Universalist Theological Situation." Library, Meadville/Lombard Theological School, Chicago. Mimeo.

————. 1971b. *25 Beacon Street and Other Recollections*. Boston: Beacon.

Meadville Theological School. 1964. *Announcement of the New Design of Theological Education at Meadville Theological School of Lombard College*. Chicago: Meadville Theological School.

Sutherland, Malcolm. 1986. Interview with author. Chicago, 11 January.

————. 1987. "Reflections on the First Twenty Years of CASIRAS: A Personal Review." *Zygon* 22 (Anniversary Issue): 20–27.

Unitarian Universalist Association. 1961. "Preliminary Reports of the Commissions of the Free Church in a Changing World." Paper presented to delegates of the Organizing Meeting of the Unitarian Universalist Association, Boston, 11–13 May. Burhoe papers. Chicago.

————. 1962. *A Comprehensive Plan of Education for the Unitarian Universalist Ministry: Complete Report of the Committee to Study Theological Education*. Boston: Unitarian Universalist Association.

————. 1963. *The Free Church in a Changing World*. Boston: Unitarian Universalist Association.

Winslow and Mae Burhoe, Ralph (with father) and Richards (with mother), in 1913.

Ralph Burhoe in 1929, hitchhiking from Boston to Chicago and return, via Louisville, Kentucky.

Frances Bickford Burhoe, Ralph's first wife, taken at the time of her Radcliffe College graduation in 1931.

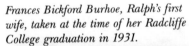

Burhoe in conversation with Hudson Hoagland, president of the Worcester Foundation for Experimental Biology, at the American Academy of Arts and Sciences offices in Brookline, Massachusetts, ca. 1960.

Celebrating the first volume of Zygon, in 1966, Burhoe, with University of Chicago president George Beadle (center), and Meadville/Lombard president Malcolm Sutherland (right).

Burhoe and Ralph Fuchs, President of the Meadville/Lombard board of directors, in front of the building that housed the various projects that Burhoe founded and directed. The house is located at 5700 South Woodlawn Avenue in Chicago; the date is 1966, coinciding with the first volume of Zygon.

From left, Burhoe, Robert Tapp, and John F. Hayward (all professors at Meadville/ Lombard) greet Kenneth Cauthen (of Colgate Rochester/Bexley Hall Theological Seminary), the first Fellow of the Center for Advanced Studies in Theology and the Sciences, in October 1977.

Burhoe receiving a Doctor of Humane Letters degree from President Thad Seymour, Rollins College, Winter Park, Florida, 1979.

Burhoe receives the Templeton Prize from Prince Philip at Buckingham Palace, 13 May 1980. From left: Sir John Templeton, Prince Philip, Mrs. Templeton, Mrs. Lynden Pindling (representing her husband, prime minister of the Bahamas), Burhoe, Calla Burhoe.

Burhoe delivering his acceptance speech for the Templeton Prize for Progress in Religion, Guildhall, London, 13 May 1980.

Ralph Wendell Burhoe and Calla Crawford Burhoe in 1986.

10 January 1986. Front row, from left: George Riggan, Burhoe, Frank Opton; back row: Karl Peters, John Godbey, Malcolm Sutherland, Calla Burhoe, Merle Riggan, Philip Hefner, Donald Szantho Harrington.

Zygon/CASIRAS Twentieth Anniversary symposium at the Lutheran School of Theology at Chicago, 10 January 1986. From left: Malcolm Sutherland, Donald Szantho Harrington, George Riggan, Burhoe.

Zygon/CASIRAS Twentieth Anniversary Symposium. From left: Don Browning, Solomon Katz, James Gustafson, William Lesher.

Zygon/CASIRAS Twentieth Anniversary Banquet at the University of Chicago Quadrangle Club, 10 January 1986. From left: Karl Peters, Marjorie Hall Davis, Solomon Katz, Nancy Houk, Lora Gross, Burhoe, George Riggan, Calla Burhoe, Merle Riggan.

9 January 1989, presentation of the Burhoe Bronze to the Chicago Center for Religion and Science. From left: sculptor John Forwalter, Burhoe, Calla Burhoe.

IV Burhoe's Theological Program

In the fall of 1964, along with the other Meadville faculty members, Burhoe was given the challenge of writing a "theological autobiography," and on 6 November 1964 he presented his paper to a faculty seminar. After tracing his development through the events that led to his joining the Meadville faculty, he wrote: "I bring with me to my professing of theology at Meadville a theology. It is not, however, a traditional theology; although I think it deals with traditional problems of theology. Moreover, it is not a finished, final, or fixed theology, although it attempts to deal with some final and ultimate questions" (Burhoe 1964d, 13–14). In making this statement, Burhoe probably felt some need to justify his selection as professor of theology and the sciences and director of the theological component of the New Design. Indeed, it is remarkable that Meadville should have selected an individual who had no formal academic degrees (let alone a formal theological education), who had worked as a meteorologist and an executive officer for a secular academy of scholars. Nevertheless, Burhoe was recognized as having the vision for developing a theological research program in the light of contemporary knowledge, as well as the gifts and talents to carry out this new effort.

Burhoe had outlined the shape of this vision in his 1959 essay "Salvation in the Twentieth Century" (see Breed 1990). There he sketched a scientific approach to religion that would lead to the formulation of a validated and salvific doctrine—a scientific theology. That essay was a summary of the the programmatic thrust of the vision that had evolved out of his work with the American Academy and especially its Committee on Science and Values. It was in the spirit of that vision, as well as his work with the Commission on Theology and the Frontiers of Learning, that Burhoe guided the founding and development of the Institute on Religion in an Age of Science (see Breed 1991). The report of the commission conveyed the essence of his vision for a theological research program and recommended the institution of such a program, whereupon Meadville included this program in its New Design and selected Burhoe to guide its development. The possibility of developing his scientific approach to religion in the training of persons for the liberal ministry provided the opportunity and challenge to develop and elaborate the theological dimension of this thought. An examination of his work in giving shape to the theology and science program at Meadville brings into focus his theological program for developing a scientific theology—the theology he brought to Meadville.

BURHOE'S INTENTION

In general, there are two approaches to the relationship of theology and contemporary thought. The first approach liberalizes traditional Christian symbols and doctrines by adding relevant scientific knowledge to their contents (see, for example, Peacocke 1979). The Christian theological tradition provides the norms and organizing vision for interpreting the contemporary intellectual environment. In the other approach, exemplified by Burhoe, new symbols and doctrines are fashioned from contemporary thought, and the traditional symbols and doctrines are related to or translated into them. Some philosophical position is usually adopted as the regulative norm and heuristic guide. For process theologians this is Whitehead's philosophy of organism. For Burhoe it is the positivism of such thinkers as Richard von Mises, Philipp Frank, and P.W. Bridgman, extended by an evolutionary worldview.

Burhoe says his theology is not traditional, even though it deals with traditional problems of theology. Because he intends to integrate science with traditional religious wisdom, the question of how the religious tradition functions in his theological program concerns us. Burhoe clearly identified himself as rooted in the Judeo-Christian tradition: "I have just presented an outline of a small part of the new breakthroughs in scientific understanding and appreciation of the wisdom of ancient and modern religion. And, like Saint Paul speaking to both Greeks and Jews, I, speaking to scientifically informed secularists and to traditional believers, appreciate both and at the same time seek to show that the views of each need to be brought together to yield a larger truth for the more effective communication to all mankind of God's sovereignty, love, and way of salvation" (Burhoe [1977] 1981, 22). However, he does not accord that tradition any special normative status:

I am convinced that the scientific methods of revealing the truth about man and the source of his being or destiny are far richer than any past programs of revelation for advancing the truth or power of life. And I find already accumulated in the several branches of the sciences a wealth of ready made revelation relevant for theology, for man's understanding of his ultimate concerns. The book of nature, or the bible of nature, as some earlier theologians called it, may add to the Judeo-Christian book or bible in revealing the glory of God (Burhoe 1964d, 22).

For the most part, Burhoe draws upon the ideas of the Judeo-Christian tradition, although he wishes not to exclude other religious traditions.

Burhoe believes that both science and religion have been selected by the same nature, system of reality, or God. Since he holds to an equivalence between the revelations of religions and the revelations of the sciences, scientific pictures of reality can illumine and lend credibility to traditional religious beliefs. The sciences are used in a religious mode to unveil what the ultimate system of powers requires. They demonstrate the validity of its evolved wisdom for human survival, and what they come up with should not conflict with what the religions themselves have revealed. Rather, the sciences will fulfill and enlarge the wisdom previously selected and embodied in the religious traditions.[1]

Burhoe says his theology is not finished, final, or fixed, although it attempts to deal with some final and ultimate questions. Because scientific knowledge of the unseen realities and processes upon which life depends is continuously growing and developing, a theology based on this knowledge would also develop and grow, and, in this sense, would never be finished, final, or fixed. As such, Burhoe's theology should be characterized by an openness to the growing body of scientifically established knowledge. However, Burhoe's theological vision and criterion of life select the most promising scientific knowledge for its relevance in meeting religious needs and solving religious problems. From this perspective, Burhoe's theology can be understood as a research program that will lead to a scientifically informed religion for which a scientific theology provides the theoretical dimension, giving direction to the continued development of the program.[2]

This chapter will examine Burhoe's conception of his program in depth, focusing on his methodology for developing a scientific approach to religion and a scientific theology. Burhoe's theological program is a significant contribution toward defining the nature of the discipline of theology and science or religion and science. The following discussion will show how the areas that Burhoe proposed for investigation, and that appeared in his proposals for a curriculum, relate to the program as a whole.

HUMAN SALVATION AND THE TASK OF A SCIENTIFIC THEOLOGY

Burhoe's theological program aims to restore the credibility of religion so as to make it socially effective and personally motivating in an age of science. Religion is essential for a viable human society because it informs society about the central values necessary for human life. Its wisdom needs to be translated into a modern idiom saturated with scientific concepts and pictures of reality. When this translation is properly made in terms of validated scientific concepts and theories, not only will the wisdom of traditional religion be validated but the scientific discoveries of reality will be valorized as revelatory of the ultimate realities upon which life depends.[3] Although Burhoe is compelled to justify to the theological community his conviction that scientific understanding is the best way toward a revitalization of religion, his primary concern is to provide recommendations, direction, and motivation for human welfare in our contemporary scientific age. Thus the starting point of Burhoe's program is to recast the problem of salvation in the context of the contemporary age of science and technology. His root concern is to reconceptualize the human situation as immersed in a rapidly changing environment, largely brought about by the power of scientific knowledge to revise, elaborate, and create new technologies. Because scientific inquiry and the technological arts have become separated from religious thought and practice, a new cultural environment has developed in which religion is merely tolerated as a relic of the past or as serving the needs of those less sophisticated; it has little real significance in the mainstream of human activity.

Some might contest the claim that the Judeo-Christian religion has lost its power in the West to science, in light of the rise of such movements as pietism in Germany or the Great Awakening in America in the eighteenth century. These movements represent an interiorization of religion within the individual. While religion may continue to be an important dimension of the spiritual life of human individuals, the interiorization or subjectivization of religion has diminished its power and effectiveness in the public realm. In fact, Burhoe observed, "The ultimate danger of . . . technological power is . . . subtle and difficult to do anything about. It threatens man's very central sense of his worth, value, meaning, purpose, direction, and will to live" (Burhoe [1964] 1966a, 125–26).

Even more subtle and threatening is the "disillusionment with the traditional formulations of religious, moral, and other value-motivating belief" that has been wrought in the new intellectual environment dominated by the sciences. Without careful attention to those ultimate values embodied in traditional religions, the "ships" of human life are in serious danger of losing their rudders and keels, and without this guidance and motivation humanity will run aground, joining other extinct species on the barrier reefs of life.

A lecture to the faculty of St. Louis University provides an example of the way Burhoe portrays the general shape of his program for dealing with this problem of salvation. "The Sciences, Humanities, and Religion—Can the Three Cultures Be Reunited?" was the keynote lecture at the President's Annual Faculty Conference in September 1964. It addressed the question of the pathway to salvation in the current fragmentation crisis in our culture: "My message to you is that the traditional curriculum content of liberal education is fast becoming obsolete for life in a new age of science. The crisis is the fragmentation of our culture into two or three or more parts and a breakdown of the organic unity of our intellectual apparatus which threatens the very life of our civilization" (Burhoe 1964c, 1). Religion has been eroded by secular challenges to religious belief, and the humanities or interpretive arts have succumbed to the same fate. "Basically, the interpretive arts are an interpretive arm of religious values, and when faith in these values fail, then the arts fall into a cry of chaos and despair" (Burhoe 1964c, 6). Because the sciences have become isolated from traditional religious concepts and images, they tend to undermine values and morality. Appealing to Arnold Toynbee and Clyde Kluckhohn, Burhoe affirmed, "No society or civilization, primitive or sophisticated, can long endure without a culture built around and integrated with a religious or value-transmitting core. If we apply this to our own society, . . . we can only conclude that our civilization is falling apart and doomed unless there is a renovation of its religious core" (Burhoe 1964c, 11).

How is this renovation to be brought about? "My proposal is that Christian scholars should be today as enterprising and flexible as the early Christian fathers, that they should become acquainted with the new 'philosophy' or worldview of the sciences, and interpret their message in its terms" (Burhoe 1964c, 14). Citing the Academy Committee on Science and Values and the work of IRAS as a promising beginning, he concluded with an appeal: "If you can feel the deep intellectual integrity and the emotional and motivational power behind such doctrines of the ground of being and man's duties and opportunities drawn from the sciences that I feel, and if you can see how closely these notions resemble some of the basic notions of the Judeo-Christian tradition, then you may wish to join with me in seeking to develop a new kind of natural theology based on the contem-

porary sciences'' (Burhoe 1964c, 18–19). A theology integrated with
the sciences can serve as the core of liberal education, because this
theology would deal with the primary or ultimate values which promote life.

Toynbee's Gifford lectures, to which Burhoe frequently refers and
upon whose insights he builds, paint a panoramic picture of the
dynamics of religion in human history (Toynbee 1956). Of particular
interest is Toynbee's perspective on the secularization of current
Western Christendom and its effect on the spiritual crisis. In the
aftermath of the breakdown of the ecumenical Western Christian
Church, spiritual allegiance was transferred to parochial secular
states. Since the seventeenth century, Toynbee notes, there has been
a psychological substitute of the pursuit of technology for the passions
of religious fanaticism, which introduced a spiritual crisis in the
midst of a burgeoning technical mastery of the mysteries of nature as
religion was replaced with technology.

Where the missionaries of Western Christianity failed (for any
number of reasons) to make converts in non-Western lands, the
technology of the West succeeded, particularly as non-Westerners
sought its new military techniques out of interest in self-defense. But
with the new technology they were forced into new life-styles reflec-
tive of the West, and with them inherited the spiritual malaise
endemic to the West. With the advent of the technical mastery of
atomic power and the specter of worldwide destruction as a consequence of a single abuse of this technology, the spiritual malaise
exploded into crisis proportions. Further, Toynbee hypothesized that
a revulsion against science and technology might develop in the later
decades of the twentieth century, comparable to the revulsion against
religion in the later decades of the seventeenth century.

Toynbee's work brings to light some of the background of
Burhoe's argument that humanity is besieged by a spiritual crisis
precipitated by the fruits of that science and technology which have
so radically changed the contours of the human landscape over the
last three hundred years. Humanity needs to be saved from this
new environment, with its threat to the religious yearning and sen-
sitivities of the human spirit and, indeed, to human life. Humanity
needs to retrieve and refashion its spiritual resources and treasures,
entrapped in premodern traditional religious forms, in order to meet
the new challenges to human life. For Burhoe, this religious revitalization is to be brought about through development of a new kind
of natural theology based on the contemporary sciences. Burhoe
takes the avenue Toynbee sees as more spiritually promising—the
scientific study of human affairs, to illumine the role of religion

in human evolution and show the validity of traditional religious wisdom.

Burhoe takes his models from evolutionary biology and applies insights from anthropology and psychology to establish the fact that religions are essential artifacts, which select, preserve, and transmit the core values in human cultural evolution. By scientifically studying religion in the context of human evolution, one can produce knowledge of those values essential for human life. A scientific theology is the theoretical formulation of those values. Theological concepts, then, receive their credibility insofar as they can be functionally related to the evolutionary process. Pursued in this fashion, theology may again become an arena for public discourse, rather than a factious enterprise concerned with parochial matters. Theology would then be dealing with public facts, whether being held accountable to the forms produced in the past by the evolutionary process or tested by its present applicability in the practices of the living religions.

The rise of Fundamentalist and conservative religious movements, especially in America, can be interpreted as responses to the loss of the effectiveness of religious values in shaping culture by retreating to traditional forms of religious expression. The interiorization of religion and its continuing effectiveness in the spiritual life of human persons does not count against Burhoe's argument, but it does raise the question whether an interpretation of religion in objective scientific terms is alone sufficient to bring about a revitalization of religion.

From a Hegelian perspective, the interiorization of religion is the dialectical counterpart to the contemplation of the universe. Turning their spiritual quest toward the heavens in a renewed contemplation of nature, natural philosophers sought to exercise their religious faith unhampered by religious fanaticism. They sought the trustworthiness of the Creator in the lawful regularities of natural phenomena, where the Creator's intentions and revelation could be found unmixed with self-centered human concerns for power and domination. They centered their spiritual quest on the radical Other —nonhuman nature. This spiritual investment in the Other, in the extreme form of Deism, reduced the human to insignificance in a deterministic, mechanical conception of the universe, and the Creator to temporal irrelevance as the utterly transcendent architect of the great world machine and its initial impetus into motion.

A romantic reaction swung 'round to pursue the spiritual quest in the radical interior of the human—the self. This radical shift in focus in the face of the threat of human insignificance in the universe, led, in the extreme of existentialism, to the denial of meaningfulness in the phenomenal external world, reducing the world to absurdity. The human self was the sole locus of order in the existential decision to live in the face of an absurd nature. The romantic reaction also brought with it the desire to reconsider human nature which blossomed into the differentiation and development of the biological and human sciences. It gave birth, in the nineteenth century, to a historical consciousness and a sensitivity to the ongoing developmental processes in human as well as nonhuman nature. With the advent of a cosmic historical consciousness, the timeworn conception of the universe as machine began to be disassembled, and the universe is becoming again an inspiring source of wonder and mystery (see Collingwood 1945).

With the rebirth of scientific cosmologies concerned with understanding the universe as a whole and constructing a theoretical conception of its history, another pathway is opening up to begin, at least intellectually, to relate God, self, and nature. A return to cosmology via the sciences is an antidote to an overly anthropocentric Christian theology and an opportunity to recover the relation of redemption to the creation as a whole (see Tracy and Lash 1985, esp. 87–91). It may allow theologians to take their place once again in the world of concrete experience, and scientists to take up again the dialogue with philosophers and theologians in order to ascertain the proper relations among the inhabitants of our cosmic home (Toulmin 1982, 16, 272). Perhaps a reconstruction of the evolutionary history of the universe and a comprehension of the processes which are involved in its ongoing development will begin to give humans a proper perspective of the whole as an interrelated cosmic drama in which humanity has an important part to play, but certainly not the most significant role.

The recovery of our cosmic heritage and the role of humanity in an evolutionary cosmos through an integration of the sciences and religion is the primary task to which Burhoe sees that theologians and scientists must address themselves if the spiritual crisis is to be resolved with a clearer understanding of the ultimate values and purposes which will sustain and continue human life.

THE DATUM OF LIFE AND THE OBJECT OF THEOLOGY

For Burhoe, life is the central category in his theological program, and religion is that institution of culture that provides the most all-embracing and fundamental integration of ideas and attitudes that move humans to behavior that makes life possible. It is because of its life-giving function that religion needs to be reformed and revitalized in the light of the sciences. This is the background for Burhoe's conviction that human survival (salvation) depends upon restoration of the credibility and efficacy of religion through integration with the knowledge and worldview of the sciences.

Theological reflection is devoted to enhancing the life-giving function of religion and to providing life-giving solutions to religious problems. It does this by focusing on the reality sacred for life—its source, sustenance, and requirements for survival. A passage from his theological-autobiographical paper illustrates this point:

> In our theological enterprise, then, I think we ought to follow the lead of such men as Tillich and push far beyond them, in focusing our attention on that which in reality is of ultimate human concern, what is in fact the reality sacred for life, what it is which in fact determines human destiny, what may be the ideas and consequent practices which in fact are required to save man from degeneration, death, and despair and lead him to higher levels of purpose, hope, and fulfillment of life. In addressing ourselves to the deeper or more abstract formulations of religious questions in a meta language, we can forget for the moment the seeming conflicts and confusions between such symbolic or conceptual systems as Christianity, Hinduism, Stoicism, Deism, Humanism, Communism, Freudianism, Existentialism, Hedonism, or Evolutionism; and begin to ask what are the real sources of the well-being of human life, its sustenance, and its salvation in an ideological framework which stands above but also includes any or all of these historic formulations (Burhoe 1964c, 15–16).

The best resource for constructing this ideological framework is the scientific evolutionary worldview and those scientifically validated theories and concepts which provide knowledge about life. The reality sacred for life, which is the object of theology and the same objective reality investigated by the sciences, selects, organizes, and validates this knowledge about life.

Burhoe's wager is that scientific knowledge of the essential nature of life will provide the best resource for guidance to full participation in life in its almost overwhelming complexity. In this wager he casts his lot with those persons who throughout human history have sought guidance for life through mystical or intellectual contemplation of nature. In the fall of 1963, at the end of his paper "New Knowledge on the Nature of Moral and Mystical Experience," he juxtaposed two quotes, one from Darwin and the other from Meister Eckhart:

> The ultimate selector and imprimatur for mystical experience and the resulting moral behavior patterns is the objective reality in which man lives and moves and has his being, reality which is truly his lord and master. All that I have been saying was said a little over a hundred years ago by Charles Darwin in one sentence: "It may be said that natural selection is daily and hourly scrutinizing, throughout the world, every variation, even the slightest; rejecting that which

is bad, preserving and adding up all that is good; silently and insensibly working, whenever and wherever opportunity offers, at the improvement of each
organic being in relation to its organic and inorganic conditions of life.''

It is interesting to note how closely Darwin's statement parallels that of the
father of German mysticism, Meister Eckhart: "Know that, by nature, every
creature seeks to become like God. Nature's intent is neither food nor drink nor
clothing nor comfort, nor anything else in which God is left out. Whether you
like it or not, secretly nature seeks, hunts, tries to ferret out the track on which
God may be found'' (Burhoe 1963, 24-25).

Writing about the many persons with whom he was associated at
the American Academy, who shared an interest in contemporary
human problems, he remarked:

Some of these men were more active in practical actions to save the world than
in theoretical problems of human salvation. We worked on atoms for peace, on
abolition of atomic war. But the men who were concerned with the theoretical
problems of the relation of science and ethics, the problems of motivating right
behavior, and the relation between various realms of knowledge and the unity of
knowledge interested me most. . . . The discussions with these groups of scientists
more than the church became for me the center of what I call my religious and
theological life (Burhoe 1965, G-8).

The knowledge of nature (the reality which sets the requirements for
and selects life), which has become formulated theoretically in the
sciences, needs to be integrated with traditional theological symbols
and concepts in order to give them credibility so they can serve as
renewed beacons or guidance for human life.

The essence of life cannot be understood on the basis of any particular manifestation of life, whether it be a biological organism, an
individual human life, or a human culture. While these particular
manifestations mediate an understanding of life, the kind of understanding Burhoe seeks to communicate is one which is applicable to
the whole of life. Burhoe is intent on getting beyond these transient
actualities to the source, destiny, and requirements for life itself. It
is the whole evolutionary history of living organisms, including their
phylogenetic history, which reveals their relative success in adapting
to their environments, which is the context for theorizing about the
nature of life. He is ultimately concerned with presenting a picture
of life in its wholeness (and the knowledge contained in and derivable
from this picture) and what it means to participate fully in life. At the
beginning of his autobiographical paper he presents the following
image:

I am now compelled to envisage my own development, including my theology,
as a complex but continuous process reaching back in time not through just a
few thousand years, but through at least a thousand thousand thousand, and
in space not only to cover the terrestrial ball but into the far reaches of the
cosmos whose history and reality [are] inseparable from mine and in whose

cosmic program of advancing life this more immediately observable entity labeled with my name is in reality a superficial phenomenon or transient phenotype of a real self which one can contemplate from modern science as well as ancient mysticism as ultimately indistinguishable from the infinite whole or one (Burhoe 1964d, 1).

This image makes it clear that although life is the datum, the object of Burhoe's theology is the infinite whole, or one, out of which all living organisms have their source and destiny as part of the cosmic program of advancing life. In addition, one must seek to apprehend the one whose primal requirements for life must be internalized as the formative values that make life possible.

Burhoe is committed to the project of providing an understanding of life from its source in cosmic reality, through the embodied instructions for life in the genetic material and in cultural artifacts, to life's phenotypic expression in a human individual. For this project evolutionary theory and the sciences, especially the human sciences, are critically important because they disclose the ever more intricate details of the processes of life, thereby revealing the conditions and requirements for life. Understanding the evolutionary thread of life is essential.

One might be tempted to say that this is only a scientific project, but Burhoe's primary aim is theological; the scientific character of the project supports the overarching goal: to relate all life to God as its source and destiny. To accomplish this goal, one must have a suitable picture, and the evolutionary worldview fills in the picture of the life to which God is related. Burhoe sees this as his own creative extension of the positivist program to which he owes a great deal, due to its influence on him (Burhoe 1966c).

Before proceeding to show the way in which Burhoe relates God to life and the methodological proposals (and their problems) arising from that endeavor, I must first discuss the picture of life that informs Burhoe's theological program. He writes:

> I would summarize this revelation of the sciences as saying that life is a system of order maintained in an environment that ordinarily decreases order and that the primary direction, goal, or value of life, which was established by the natural selection that is an inherent characteristic of the general environment, is to continue that order or, in the history of evolutionary development, to increase that order. . . . One could say that life was created by, and its primary goal or value is forever established by, the nature of the cosmos. . . . It is the task of all evolving systems of life to explore further routes to this primary goal as challenged by the ever changing circumstances set forth by the environment. . . .
>
> . . . A wide scientific community seems to see this negentropic or order-building goal as the primary good or value of life, running as a common thread from the primitive organic chemicals to the highest religions (Burhoe 1967, 78–80).

Burhoe continues this description of the "common thread" of life through five steps of "man's history of learning to know right from wrong and good from evil": genotypic knowledge, the brain's knowledge, culturally transmitted knowledge, rational knowledge, and scientific knowledge.

Another point needs to be emphasized. Burhoe's picture of life is a creative construction painted from the vast conceptual resources of the sciences. Furthermore, it is a creative construction oriented to the service of his theological project.

> . . . If we love humanity and if we stand in awe and love before the majesty and wonder of the handiwork and purpose of the creator of life on earth, we must commit ourselves assiduously to the labors of abstracting the religiously relevant and necessary truths inherent, but not necessarily manifest, in the revelations of the sciences. As one of our spiritual ancestors, Ralph Waldo Emerson, has said, we need not at first be concerned with writing the songs but with elaborating the vital truth; as soon as they see it the poets and musicians will provide the corresponding songs for more widespread communication (Burhoe 1964d, 24).

As this passage points out, the picture of life Burhoe constructs is an abstraction of the religiously relevant truth from the resources of the sciences. This does not mean, however, that Burhoe is launching into poetry or metaphysical speculation. Seeking to avoid the charges leveled against such endeavors as Teilhard's, he intends to remain within the arena of scientific discourse and its refining fire for winnowing out the truth.

Conceived in this spirit of openness to the sciences without sacrificing the integrity of the theological task, Burhoe's program opens the door to seeing the vital relationship and mutuality of a wide range of researchers. Scientists have an essential role in the project, because they are involved in producing knowledge which is potentially of high relevance for developing a unified picture of life, and also because they are needed to contribute to the testing of the hypotheses generated to construct such a unified picture. Theologians have an essential role in discerning the religious and theological relevance of particular pieces of scientific knowledge for understanding the relationship of life, elaborated scientifically, to God, the source and creator of life, by drawing on the vast resources of religious and theological traditions. Finally, there is the essential role of the scientific theologian (or the theological scientist) who labors creatively to construct a scientific picture of life in relation to God, venturing proposals to be tested for their validity and spiritual efficacy by scientists and theologians, as well as by all humans seeking to embody the religious life in the contemporary age.

Since there is no single text that presents the picture of life in its entirety, Burhoe ranks as a creative theoretical scientist (or, more traditionally, a natural philosopher) who seeks to unify disparate scientific knowledge into a general conception of the process of life. In this he is continuing the project of the unified sciences, which is part of the formative legacy of ideas Burhoe imbibed under the tutelage of Philipp Frank.

Since Burhoe's picture of life is an assumption, as well as a result of his research, it is most difficult to get hold of. It is only from bits and pieces, located in the course of his arguments on various topics, that this picture of life can be given the differentiated specificity that I have described. Nonetheless, it is because his picture of life so permeates his thought as a given totality that life can be considered to be the primary datum of Burhoe's theological program. His criterion for judging whether a scientific resource is religiously or theologically relevant is whether it illumines the datum of life. Such scientific ideas as quantum theory, relativity theory, astrophysical theories of the Big Bang, and evolution of the physical universe have not warranted significant attention in Burhoe's thought because, in his judgment, they are too remotely related to an understanding of life.[4]

The Idea of God and the Metaphysics of Physics

Our interpretation of the way in which the idea of God, the object of theology, is the regulative and organizing principle in Burhoe's program begins with a discussion of his lectures on the "Metaphysics of Physics." These lectures, given in January 1964, during his consideration as the person to guide the theology and science component of the New Design at Meadville, were an extension of Burhoe's Meadville lectures of 1961 (see Breed 1991). They dealt with the theological agenda of Burhoe's vision, which he had outlined at the end of his "Salvation in the 20th Century."

In the first of three lectures he outlined the metaphysical basis of his program in three propositions about how the God concept is related to the new form and character being given to traditional metaphysics by contemporary physics. In the second and third lectures he discussed two additional propositions by adding to physics those implications for metaphysics stemming from biology, especially evolutionary theory. These five propositions are the core of his theological program, and we will look at their detail to see how they generated specific problem areas, to be explored, elaborated, and solved.

The selection of these propositions was based on his faith in God, for in the conclusion he says, "I truly worship this majestic cosmic reality or god. . . . For me god is not dead, but terribly and wonderfully real" (Burhoe 1964d, 24). This theocentric perspective is also at the heart of his criteria for selecting the propositions:

The theological topics I propose to take up are not necessarily related in any one-to-one way with topics in traditional theology. I have picked them rather (1) because they seem to me to be particularly important for salvation today, and (2) because I happen to have seen a way of making good sense of them in terms of the contemporary sciences (Burhoe 1964a, 8).

The first of these criteria may be called the *criterion of religious* (or *theological*) *relevance,* and the second the *criterion of scientific connectability* (which has to do with establishing the validity of religious or theological ideas by connecting them to validated scientific concepts and ideas).[5]

THE CONCEPT OF METAPHYSICS

A metaphysics of physics is the ground for constructing the connection between science and religion. However, Burhoe is aware of the fact that, in the criticism of logical positivism, metaphysics is often understood to be unscientific. "Today, the worlds of science and scholarship hardly recognize the term *metaphysics,* and if they do it is a bad word, to be avoided." Even though Burhoe understands and intends metaphysics to be the primary bridge-building material, because of his belief in this misunderstanding of metaphysics, he either distances himself in his writing from metaphysics or avoids the term altogether. In the lectures considered here, given largely to a private and theological audience, he directly discusses how metaphysics can be the primary material for the bridge. His intention is to revise traditional metaphysics in terms of contemporary physical concepts. In this way metaphysics could be given a new credibility, because by doing metaphysics in terms of the concepts and practices of physics, the logical-positivist objection that metaphysical statements are not empirically testable would be overcome.

Rather than reject the function of traditional metaphysics, Burhoe pursued the question "what it was that metaphysics really intended to study," and for this he turned to Aristotle.

Following Aristotle, metaphysics was the First Philosophy or Theology, and was concerned with such things as were denoted by the terms *ontology,* meaning the real or ultimate nature of the reality underlying that which is experienced or observed; *cosmology,* meaning the ultimate order, causal connections, or processes explaining the events experienced or observed; and *theology,* meaning the prime mover or ultimate cause of the events we experience. It is only natural to suppose that any investigation of the ultimate or most general characteristics of the real natures and causes of things should lead to conceiving entities which are not directly sensible, and hence that metaphysics should come to denote the science of the supersensible, the invisible, or supernatural world. Since the time of Descartes, the term *metaphysics* also became increasingly involved with the problem of how we know, *epistemology* [emphasis added].

Physics, as extended to include the whole range of the natural sciences, "has revolutionized our notions of ontology, cosmology, and epistemology."

Because physics is the new metaphysics, revolutionizing and restoring credibility to ontology, cosmology, and epistemology, this new metaphysics can also revolutionize and restore credibility to theology:

In the term *physics,* I mean our concept of all nature as we may know it from all disciplines, and not just a narrow band of disciplines, such as geometry, kinetics, and mechanics. It includes most of what today is called *science,* which is a set of conceptual systems largely interlocking with physics, including biophysics and psychophysics.

Physics, then, extended to include the natural sciences, can serve to restore credibility by providing the connectability between the world of the senses and the world of unseen and hidden realities, lacking in traditional metaphysics (Burhoe 1964a, 3–7).

A quote from a memorandum on "Theology and the Sciences at Meadville" will help illustrate this point.

The task of integrating the sciences with religion is very complex and delicate and involves many areas of the sciences and many aspects of life and man's understanding of the nature of life. Most religions, cultures, and scientific systems have evolved to complexly integrated structures without people being very conscious of what is going on. . . .

This complexity, and the need for an integrated (internally self-consistent map or view of the way things are, the scientific equivalent of "metaphysics") worldview, if one is to be able to use the conceptual system with any reliability or effectiveness, means that a person is either required to understand or, if not fully to understand, then at least to accept some coherent conceptual system of the world and man on faith in the scientific community the way people accept some scientific conceptual system about atomic energy or moon flights. . . .

Therefore, a first requisite for a scientifically based theology is a new "metaphysics" that conforms to some coherent scientific worldview of the way things are, including man, his world, and the history or the dynamics in time of that system. Only when built upon such a "metaphysics" can one say that one has a scientific doctrine of human salvation, a scientifically informed theology. This "metaphysics" must include . . . the realm of values as well as the realm of facts (Burhoe 1969, 11–12).

For Aristotle, science concerned that knowledge which could be proved by demonstration, reasoning from wide generalities or common beliefs to particular results, according to the rules of deductive logic. Wisdom, or philosophy, concerned itself with the discernment of the proper starting points for demonstration using the method of dialectics. His *Metaphysics* dealt with wisdom, or knowledge of the most general principles and causes of things, which he called the *science of substance* or *being as such*. In a passage on the relation of the three theoretical sciences (physics, mathematics, and theology), Aristotle argued that theology is the "first" science because it deals with the highest genus of being (that which is immovable and separate). He then posed the question whether theology is universal or deals with one genus or kind of being. "We answer that if there is no substance other than those which are formed by nature, natural science will be the first science; but if there is an immovable substance, the science of this must be prior and must be first philosophy, and universal in this way, because it is first" (Aristotle *Metaphysics* vi.1.1026^{b}25).

With the revolutions in physical conceptuality in the beginning of the twentieth century, informed by the integration of physical knowledge in the nineteenth, the Aristotelian idea of substance, essence, or the being of a thing was transformed into the conceiving of things in terms of invariant physical constants and laws of proportional relations. The slow process of thought from the Copernican revolution (a moving earth), through Newton (everything moving in an absolute space), to Einstein (the elimination of any absolute frame of reference) has shattered the belief in an immovable first substance. Recent cosmology has likewise shattered the belief that this first substance can be thought to be separate from the cosmos, let alone considered to be a substance at all. "Evaporation" of the immovable and separate substance conceptually removed theology from consideration as one of the theoretical sciences, contrary to Aristotle's reasoning. By the beginning of the twentieth century mathematical physics had become the epitome of scientific method and the yardstick against which to measure the other sciences. The three theoretical sciences of Aristotle were collapsed into one, integrating physics and mathematics and eliminating theology. In this sense, mathematical physics has succeeded theology as the "first philosophy" and assumed the role of a new metaphysics. Under the positivist interpretation, a philosophy based on this physics will progressively isolate "an ever more comprehensive realm of thought that is kept free from metaphysics, and in which *connectible* descriptions of the phenomena vital to man are sought" (Mises 1951, 362).

By saying that physics has produced a new metaphysics upon which to base theology, Burhoe can be and has been interpreted as reducing theology to physics. This criticism is partially justified and certainly points out the dangers of such an approach; however, on at least two grounds this criticism misses the mark. First, the metaphysics (scientific myth or scientific worldview) upon which Burhoe builds is more concerned with the biological sciences and evolutionary theory than with mathematical physics (which he assumes in general but does not elaborate). Second, Burhoe engages in metaphysical thought with the intention to connect (in the positivistic sense of the term) God and the world, subjectivity and objective reality, and the facts of experience and the values that promote life.

One would better criticize Burhoe for not paying enough attention to the structure of the bridge. By this I mean that Burhoe does not give enough attention to critical reflection on the mode of rationality he has adopted for its construction, namely, that of later positivism. This may be excused, however, for one may become paralyzed by being too self-conscious in the act of building. Burhoe does not ground his concepts in discussions of philosophy.[6] Rather, he builds from assumed general concepts in a positivistically interpreted science, selecting those beliefs of scientists most worthy of speculation and most relevant to the religious problems of salvation.

Burhoe's intention is to be scientific in his method, and this means building theology out of the theoretical material of physics and biology, much as physical and biological theory are built out of hypotheses generated from and tested by empirical data. On this analogy, Burhoe's procedure is a scientific dialectic of theology with the theories and models of sciences and *not* the philosophy of the sciences, as the sciences are in a dialectic of theories with the data of experience, observation, experiments, and measurements. His procedure is to abstract credible and testable general concepts from the sciences that can be related to traditional theological concepts and to translate (or operationalize) theological concepts in terms of the abstracted scientific concepts. This puts his theological concepts at risk, because they are dependent upon the theories of the sciences, and because theories of science are open to change, theology is opened to revision. To establish the credibility of theology in relation to the sciences on this procedure is to establish the connectability of its concepts to scientific theories and models which are in principle connectable to empirical experience. Thus a theology built on and tested by physical theory is in principle connected to empirical experience and hence scientific—and, of course, vulnerable to the changing theories of the sciences.

The value of this kind of approach is that it provides an interdependence of theology and the sciences, as well as a means by which theological constructions can be tested, corrected, and grow with the sciences. There is the danger that if, for the sake of credibility, theological construction is restricted to this procedure, other methodologies may be dismissed as having little relevance or credibility for showing the relation of human experience to its sacred source, let alone exercising a critical function in theological construction. Burhoe has been criticized for not giving sufficient attention to the aesthetic and the demonic dimensions, as well as history.[7] He claims, however, to have done so. Although he has explained aesthetics, the demonic, and history in terms of natural selection, physical principles, and the neurophysiological operation of the brain, alternative approaches have not been critically assessed, except to say in general that they are beholden to a prescientific worldview. By not critically engaging alternative forms of thought, Burhoe's program not only loses persuasiveness but also runs the risk of an outcome opposite to that intended—as pointed out by Viggo Mortensen: "Burhoe's intention of revitalizing religion by integrating God into the sciences could actually, against his intentions, lead to the abolishment of religion. When religion can be explained as a mere manifestation of brain functions, and God can be explained by genetics, then religion becomes nothing but words, words that we could just as well do without" (Mortensen 1985).

Mortensen, however, misses the essential contribution of Burhoe's theory of religion. For Burhoe, religion is never mere words; it is that aspect of culture which accumulates and transmits ultimate values for human survival. Theology may be mere words, but not religion. Nonetheless, the point still holds, for if the values of religion are conveyed to subsequent generations through words and symbols, and those words and symbols are replaced with contemporary scientific words and symbols, it could well be the case that essential religious values would be lost.

THE CONCEPT OF GOD

The logical-positivist claim that theology and metaphysics are nonsense because their statements cannot be connected to empirical experience is addressed by Burhoe's first proposition:

Proposition 1. There is a god, if by that term we mean to designate the source of what we experience. . . . God, thus defined, is the main preoccupation of physics: to discover the source or cause of anything we experience. . . . The reality of such a God, a causal or at least correlatable system of events, is the basic postulate of physics.

God, the source of what we experience, is the reality with which we are ultimately connected in an interrelated web of events.

The [basic postulate of physics] may be stated more or less as follows: Any event of our experience can potentially be logically related or explained in terms of other events. The postulate asserts that there is nothing which inherently forbids expanding the conceptual linkages ad infinitum until all events are bound together in a single interrelated net. This net is not broken and knows no absolute boundaries between physics, chemistry, biology, psychology, sociology, or any area of experience or observation [including history, private experiences, those outside the world we see and hear, and memory]. In a sense this net of usually invisible forces or entities connecting or interrelating the diverse elements of the phenomena of human experience, which is postulated by physics and is increasingly found in fact to be interconnected into a single whole, may be said to be today's formulation of the God concept (Burhoe 1964a, 8–9).

Formulating the concept of God in this way, Burhoe shows the deep roots of his thought in the positivistic philosophy of science represented by Richard von Mises. For example, compare the above with the following quotations from the conclusion of von Mises's *Positivism:*

The goal of all scientific endeavor is to discover connections between observable phenomena, such that out of a partially given complex the remaining elements can be constructed in thought.

... Progress of research leads in every sphere away from metaphysics, toward the realm of connectible scientific theories.

... The religious systems are metaphysical attempts at an explanation of the world, undertaken for the purpose of setting up norms of behavior. We expect from the future that to an ever-increasing extent scientific knowledge, i.e., knowledge formulated in a connectible manner, will control life and the conduct of men (Mises 1951, 369–70).

Burhoe goes on to say that it is out of our experience that we have been building our knowledge, including abstract representations in language and especially those of mathematical physics. "The network of interconnection of the scientifically formulated entities and laws relating them has indeed built up a wonderful portrait of the human situation: of man and man's relation to the more immediate ground of his being in the cosmos." While physics does not provide certain knowledge about the ultimate reality, it seems "to be saying that such a God is partially but increasingly knowable. . . . To experience increasing levels of proximate knowledge which evolves cumulatively is both thrilling in its own right and fruitful in its use." This points to the context of a major problem to which Burhoe devotes extensive attention: the connection of knowledge through its evolutionary stages from the source of what we experience to the most abstract scientific formulations and the way in which this reality selects or determines viable knowledge (Burhoe 1964a, 10–11).

Burhoe judges that this concept of God is too abstract and remote from the human predicament to be of much concern to religious theory:

The only validity of this concept may be its reality. But it is this reality which is of utmost importance, and of which we must not let go. It is upon this reality that I want to build the rational and empirical chains that bring such a god to the human predicament. . . . In fact it is the reality of the god of physics that has caused the death of other gods in populations into which education has brought the beliefs of the sciences, and this happened first in Christendom (Burhoe 1964a, 12).

In this passage we can see the basis for his later statements, in which he identifies God and nature. Consider, for example, the following passage from his "Concepts of God and Soul":

Many will be disturbed by the seeming impropriety of my using the term *God* as the totality of the natural world rather than as a being beyond nature, a supernatural being. . . . Let me say that one can interpret the ancient usage of "supernatural" as referring to a hidden "nature" which is just as "real" as the tangible, visible world "out there" which everyone can see. Hence, "supernatural" means essentially the hidden, subtle forces not immediately obvious to common sense. During the past few centuries the changes in physics have quite obliterated this distinction between nature and supernature (Burhoe 1973, 423).[8]

This identification of God and nature, or the natural and the supernatural, "works" if nature is conceived as the interconnected web of reality indicated above. In his program to translate traditional theological and metaphysical concepts into a physicalistic (connectable) language based on the concepts of contemporary physics, Burhoe is seeking to articulate a scientific monism in contrast to the kinds of dualisms that arise when nature is identified with one side of such distinctions as natural-supernatural, nature (essence)-thing, mind-matter, subject-object, fact-value, Creator-creature. If nature is identified with only one side of these contrasts, as in many traditional views, the identification breaks down.

Burhoe's second proposition is an answer to the question of dualism. It would be better classed as a lemma, for it is implicit in his first proposition.

Proposition 2. It should be clear that this ground of being pictured by physics is single, one, universal. There are not two or more separate networks of causality. . . . The faith that one can find a single relatively simple logical expression of the operation of the causal network is well known in the story of Albert Einstein's search for a unified field theory (Burhoe 1964a, 12).

Burhoe illustrates how this monism deals with the problem of consciousness—the estrangement of self from an objective other. He claims to have "avoided the impasse between subjective and objective by defining god and the causal network of physics as 'the source of what we experience' rather than of 'what we see' or of 'what in reality is going on out there.'" Burhoe affirms a position which embraces the alleged solipsism of the physicist P. W. Bridgman without rejecting the behaviorism of Skinner, who resolves the dualism by denying consciousness or mind. Without exhausting the concept of consciousness as the percipient subject to which experience is related, "such things as vision, hearing, feeling, emotion, love, hate, fear, etc." can be accounted for as physical processes "to be described in terms of electrical, chemical, and related processes in the neural net that makes the brain." This idea, that the brain is the locus of human integration of the experiences, given by the "source of what we experience," and that consciousness can be described in physicalistic terms, is one of the central problems to which Burhoe gives considerable attention in his later writings. "It is interesting to see how close this is to the religious mystics who assert their oneness with and inseparability from all being or god" (Burhoe 1964a, 13).

In his third proposition, Burhoe turns to the problem of linking his "god of physics" to the traditional concept of God the Creator:

Proposition 3. This god of the metaphysics of physics is the Creator, the source of all that is, including the living as well as the non-living. . . . By creator we mean that for any event or system of events at the present moment there is some antecedent condition which determined it (Burhoe 1964a, 14).

This proposition could be called a theorem of cosmic causality, for it connects the traditional notions of God's creativity to the physical principle of causality. Because it introduces the dimension of time, causality can be considered the physical analogue of history. "Without claiming touch with the ultimate, science today can carry several lines of the history of genesis back in time. . . . Perhaps the most important feature of this scientific quest for the ultimate ground of being is that it seems to be convergent rather than divergent." Burhoe notes the parallel of the emerging scientific cosmology with the creation story which informs the Judeo-Christian tradition (Burhoe 1964a, 14–15).

A perennial theological problem with the idea of the world as God's creation is theodicy. In the face of evil and death, how can God be considered to be a God of justice? Burhoe discusses this problem in relation to the second law of thermodynamics. If, according to the second law, life and order are doomed by the ultimate degradation of available energy, does not this imply that the cosmos of physics is no respecter of the human? In spite of the presumption that, with certain assumptions, the ultimate future of the universe may be a "heat death," there is a more positive implication in thermodynamic theory, and Burhoe quotes Harlow Shapley: "The natural emergence of living organisms in the early history of the earth now seems to have been not only possible but inevitable" (Shapley 1963, 57). He continues, "Life is not a freak element of the cosmos. The cosmos creates life. The evolution of life is a natural consequence of the cosmic realities and the cosmic laws." Burhoe also draws upon Schrödinger's *What Is Life?* to elaborate the point: Life is a natural consequence of a cosmos ruled by the second law, although it runs counter to the direction predicted by that law. Indeed, this is one of the important arguments in Burhoe's development of his program (Burhoe 1964a, 18–21).

Burhoe summarizes the religious value of his program for a translation of theology and metaphysics into physicalistic concepts connectible with the sciences.

In summary, the new genesis, the new creation story, tells us that life and man are created and nourished, sustained and guided by the one and only source of all that is, the almighty, unchanging, eternal sovereign of the cosmos and determiner of destiny. . . .

If traditional theologians could accept the contemporary sciences and clothe them in proper religious garb or interpretations as did the Psalmists, then this new physics, this new revelation of the prime-mover, the ultimate ground of being, the eternal, omnipotent, unchanging, ubiquitous, creator, sustainer, and ruler of all that is, would be an asset instead of a liability in presenting the moral and spiritual message of salvation. God would be real again, not dead. Moreover, preachers could say "thus saith the Lord" and be listened to with the same respect accorded to the scientifically grounded physician.

Burhoe then quotes passages from Psalms 19, 1, 139, 95, and ends with: "This religious poetry is vitally true according to the metaphysics of physics; and one can resonate to the depths of one's soul as I do, hearing these words in the context of contemporary physical theory" (Burhoe 1964a, 21–24).

This first lecture shows the basic epistemological, ontological, and cosmological principles of Burhoe's theological program. The other two lectures in the series "Metaphysics of Physics" focus on his axiology and anthropology:

In this second lecture I wish to stimulate your thinking in a not very common or well-established pattern today—a pattern which says (1) that this invisible, eternal reality portrayed by physics is the source and sanction of our moral law; and (2) that man himself is much more than the mortal corpus or the transient existential feeling that the untutored perception seems to represent; he is in reality an immortal soul or spirit, endowed by the Creator with powers, duties, and privileges in carrying on the creative process of the kingdom to come (Burhoe 1964b, 1).

The manuscripts of these second and third lectures are much more sketchy than his first, and in them he ventures into the more speculative dimension of his program, to include morals and human motivation. In keeping to his method of connecting traditional religious ideas with a physicalistic description, he must rely on the biological sciences and the more controversial concepts of the psychosocial sciences, especially those of cultural evolution. He is therefore pressed to be more of a constructive scientific theoretician, and consequently these areas are primary in development of his program.

In "The Source and Sanction of Our Moral Law," Burhoe proposes to unify natural and moral law through his concept of God. "The Lord who guides the stars in their courses is the same who counseleth the heart of man" (Burhoe 1964b, 2). The cosmic (natural and moral) law is conceived as the set of conditions for existence and life in terms of a continuous spectrum of right and wrong choices.

I can roughly characterize this spectrum of right and wrong choices as being synonymous with the building of living systems. Right structure or behavior produces life; wrong structure or behavior annihilates life. . . . [Kant] did not know what we now know about the building up of the moral law within by the objective, external selective agents, which codified these cosmically approved rules for feeling and behaving in the genotypes and culturetypes of men, in a process continuing throughout millions of generations and starting billions of years before anything recognizable as man appeared on earth (Burhoe 1964b, 3-5).

Human moral and spiritual laws are a special case of the total cosmic law which has created all life and all other things in the universe (Burhoe 1964b, 17).

The physical basis for life which underlies all human values is suggested by physicist R. B. Lindsay's "thermodynamic imperative" to consume disorder (entropy), replacing disorder with order. In evolutionary theory, natural selection is the concept used to designate the "agency weeding out the unfit or taboo patterns" and thus promoting life. For B. F. Skinner, operant reinforcement resembles natural selection in selecting individual behavior patterns. Although the evidence is not yet fully clear, a similar selection process, according to invariant laws, seems to operate in cultural evolution.

This mechanism [natural selection] is tantamount to God's will. It does the things traditionally ascribed to the gods. The important point here is that such a selector is the source of moral codes and religious beliefs. . . .

That our basic cosmic reality partially revealed by physics is the source of all truth or commands defining right and wrong behavior, that this reality not only defines and teaches us this truth but enforces it with inescapable vigilance, gives our cosmic god some of the religious relevance of the Old Testament God of the Judeo-Christian tradition (Burhoe 1964b, 17–18).

This, the predominant theme of Burhoe's theological program, is illustrated by the title of a later essay, "Natural Selection and God," where in the opening sentence he says: "One of the prime elements of a scientifically grounded theology is the rebirth or renewal of credibility in an objective reality that determines human destiny" (Burhoe 1972, 30).

THE CONCEPT OF SOUL

Having discussed the external, objective cosmic law of life which both creates and sustains viable organisms, Burhoe in the last lecture, "Image of God or Soul," turned to the human locus of cosmic evolution. The human is the locus of integration of physical, biological, and cultural selective processes governed by the cosmic law or natural selection. "I want to say something about the physics of man's soul or spirit" (Burhoe 1964b, 19). The concept of soul is concerned with understanding the emotional and psychological dimensions of humanity, and most particularly hope and motivation, on the basis of something which transcends the individual human body. He referred to his 1951 paper in which he first proposed a trinitarian concept of soul as the integration of biological (genotype), cultural (culturetype), and environmental (cosmotype) factors into a phenotypic expression of a human being.

The most obvious physicalistic dimension is the genotype, which determines not only physical development but also behaviors, chief among them being those that ensure its continuance through procreation. However, immortality is not solely dependent on passing one's genes to one's children. The genes which make up the individual genotypic structure are distributed among the whole human population in a gene pool that can be described according to stochastic and statistical laws:

My genetic elements are all over the place, not just in me. But in addition to the gene pool there are other elements of the anatomy or physical structure of the soul that also endure from as far as we can see in the distant past to the distant future, such as the culturally transmitted patterns of structure and behavior and the cosmic ground that backs the intertwined evolution of the genotypic and cultural patterns in human life. We have solid, physical grounds today for religious theories or theologies of an immortal soul.

It is clear from the physical analysis that the real values or treasures in living systems are located in this hitherto invisible or unanalyzed reality that I choose to call the soul. This is the soul of a species of animals, the heart and core of every individual. This structure does not come into being nor pass away with the birth and death of the body. With the eye of a scientist one can view the succession of phenotypes (somata, or bodies as we call them) appearing and disappearing on an everlasting chain of the genotype and other components of the soul (Burhoe 1964b, 25–26).

On this view, one must give up the idea of some traditional views of immortality that there is a continuation of consciousness after the death of the body: "For physics there is no continuation of the consciousness, the feeling, the sensing, the seeing, the thinking, the satisfactions of life apart from the bodily base that produces [these effects]. The disembodied spirit doesn't exist. . . . Our immortal spirits, although quite invisible and intangible, are nevertheless embodied and real" (Burhoe 1964b, 27).

In conclusion, he says,

In this picture is revealed to us the apparatus that motivates our basic concern for the welfare of the species, a value we hold dearer than the lives of our bodies; that motivates our strivings to bring about the will of the Creator as well as provides our basic understanding and our deep respect for our Creator's eternal laws, which in fact are built into our very being—created in his own image, as the old Genesis said (Burhoe 1964b, 28b).

I hope that some of you see some validity in my suggestion that one can build up a religiously relevant doctrine of soul on these revelations of reality from physics, a doctrine which has the psychological, emotional, and motivational equivalents of the older religious metaphysics which we have had to call obsolete and inadequate for informed people in today's world (Burhoe 1964b, 29).

For Burhoe, the soul is the everlasting stream of life, a stream of viable information from which individual organisms receive their heritage and to which they contribute their naturally selected patterns for life. By selecting individual organisms for their viability, nature is ultimately operating on the soul to fashion the evolution of humanity. It is for this reason that a number of problems have an essential place in Burhoe's program.

Methodologically, the problem of the fact and value distinction is important. Burhoe devotes much attention to arguing the idea that values are a class of facts, provided by selective pressures for viability in a specific environment. Values are theoretically comprehended in terms of a system of laws which describe the way in which the conditions of a specific environment regulate the evolution of life, the development of individual organisms, and the maintenance of living systems. Values are conceptually apprehended in terms of symbols which represent the accumulated information about the requirements of the environment for viability. Also, values are accumulated in the genotype, and socially learned values are accumulated in the brain. A living organism may be ontologically considered to be the expression of a viable set of values which determine its being, what it is, and how it functions in its environment. Developing this concept of value as a class of facts is essential to affirm that the scientific study of values is not alien to scientific inquiry and that a scientific study of religion is both possible and necessary because the phenomenon of religion is the source of ultimate values for human life.

A second set of problems deals with the connection between physical laws and the organic locus of their applicability. To warrant the claim that God is the creator of life, Burhoe needs to show how physical laws conspire to produce the values they inspire to ordain the creation of ever more complex ordered entities and living organisms. There cannot be some kind of vital force that creates life in the midst of nonliving stuff which is not itself explainable in terms of physical laws. Life must be shown to have continuity with the same principles which regulate the nonliving processes.[9]

A third set of problems has to do with the interaction of genes and culture. How far do genes (structural elements of the individual genotype encoded in DNA molecules) determine the behavioral and social patterns of humans, as well as other animals and living systems? Does the development of a culturetype (composed of transmitted memories of such behaviors and social patterns) react with the gene pool of a particular culture, thereby changing the stochastic and statistical distributions of genes in it or modifying the expression of genes in patterns of greater viability? Burhoe quotes a suggestive passage from B. F. Skinner in this regard: "Cultural practices which are advantageous will tend to be characteristic of the groups which survive and which therefore perpetuate those practices. Some cultural practices may therefore be said to have survival value, while others are lethal in the genetic sense" (Burhoe 1964b, 16). This set of problems is especially important in the subsequent development of Burhoe's argument that religions are an essential component in human evolution.

A related problem concerns the hypothesis (which Burhoe later advances) that belief in God promotes the selection of those patterns of human behavior which make civilization possible:

The religious gods of the life-explaining myths are themselves the naturally selected symbols which effectively motivated within the brain structures of those times the suitable response patterns to the realities that were in fact the creators and determiners of human destiny as now understood scientifically (Burhoe 1979, 156).

Although this idea is elaborated a decade later—after Burhoe was introduced to such research as that of George C. Williams through his association with Donald T. Campbell—its germ was already present at this time in relation to his operational definition of moral law:

By moral behavior I mean behavior that is commonly designated as right or wrong, good or bad, especially as the behavior may involve relations with other persons. The moral character of behavior is often considered to be accented when it involves the sacrifice of some goals of the actor in order to achieve the goals of others, and is the more sharply accented the more aware the actor is of this situation and the greater his sacrifice (Burhoe 1963, 2).

Burhoe's hypothesis raises a number of scientifically interesting questions. Can a belief in higher gods have a significant enough influence on either the gene pool or on the mechanisms of selecting social behavior patterns to warrant the viability of the hypothesis that such a belief increases altruism to nonkin individuals? What kinds of adaptive advantages would such a belief give to a human population? In the evolution of different cultures, what would account for the different contents of this belief in higher gods? Are some of these beliefs more adaptive than others?

More to the point, however, is a note in his "Cosmic Evolutionary Creation and Christian God":

This hypothesis is crucial for my account of human nature since, without symbiosis of the human gene pool with an independently selected but highly coadapted culturetype, and the role of religion in bonding the gene pool to the culturetype, *Homo* could not have become altruistically cooperative beyond close kin, and hence civilized (Burhoe 1984, 246).

The heuristic guidance toward the clear articulation of this hypothesis is rooted in Burhoe's faith in God as it is here expressed in his "Metaphysics of Physics." If God is the source of what we experience; if this source of what we experience is a single, universal network of causality of which we are an experiencing subject; if the source is the antecedent condition which determines the present; if life is not a highly improbable accident, but is the natural consequence of the cosmic reality and its laws; if life, and especially human life, is created, nourished, sustained, and guided by the one and only source of all that is, the almighty, unchanging, eternal, sovereign of the cosmos, and determiner of destiny; if this God is the source and sanction of our moral law and the selector of the right patterns for life; if the human is an epiphenomenon of the soul of life created by God in the evolution of living systems governed by natural selection, an epiphenomenon appearing and disappearing on an everlasting chain of the genotype and other components of the soul; and if identification with this soul motivates our basic concern for the welfare of the species, a value we hold dearer than the lives of our bodies; then belief in this God should make a difference in human evolution. If it could be shown that belief in God has had an essential role in human cultural evolution, we would be warranted to say that belief in God today will make a difference in human life. For Burhoe, belief in God, conceptually formulated in terms of the contemporary scientific worldview, will make a difference. The salvation of one's soul depends upon our respect for, discernment of, and abiding by the eternal laws or will of God.

This hypothesis, that belief in a transhuman reality or god, cultivated in the evolution of religions, has made human civilization possible by culturally transforming inherent genetic selfishness, puts religious belief in God at risk.[10] If, upon careful scientific analysis, such a hypothesis (or revision of it) cannot be confirmed as a possibility, then not only would disconfirmation count against the hypothesis but also would bring about serious doubt as to the efficacy of any religious belief in God.

In summary, then, the metaphysics of physics shows clearly the concept of God to which Burhoe related his exegesis of the scriptures of the sciences and around which his integration of religion and science was organized into a scientific theology. In brief, Burhoe's concept of God can be stated as follows: There is one God who is sovereign over the whole universe, and the purpose of the human is to recognize this God as "lord and master" and to spend all one's days in discovering and applying what God indicates must be done if one is to have life and more abundant life.

NOTES

1. This argument was clarified by Burhoe's response to an earlier draft, expressed to the author in a memo of 31 March 1988.

2. The concept of a research program is drawn from Imre Lakatos (see Lakatos 1978). According to Lakatos's methodology, the great scientific achievements are research programs. In the history and philosophy of science, he asserts, the basic unit of appraisal should be, not an isolated theory or a conjunction of theories, but a research program. Such a program has a *hard core,* which is metaphysical in character and by provisional decision is irrefutable, and a *positive heuristic,* which defines the construction of a belt of auxiliary hypotheses that interpret known facts or predict new ones. A research program is progressive as long as its theoretical growth anticipates its empirical growth. It becomes stagnant when its theoretical growth lags behind its empirical growth.

3. In his 1977 response to critics of his "Lord of History" essay (Burhoe 1975), Burhoe affirms that his enterprise centers in his effort to valorize scientific understanding in religious terms and to validate religious understanding in scientific terms (Burhoe 1977, 374).

4. This is not to suggest that they remain outside the scope of his project, for he has recently admired the work of Eric Chaisson in elaborating this relationship, as he

admired the work of Harlow Shapley and George Wald (see Chaisson 1979). Nonetheless, he is skeptical of cosmological theories of the origins of the universe and their usefulness for theology, because of their speculative character and lack of empirical confirmation.

5. Cf. Philipp Frank's scientific and philosophical criteria of truth (Frank 1957, esp. 18).

6. For example, see Capek 1961; Koyre 1957.

7. See the articles by W. Widick Schroeder, John Miles, Donald Musser, and Philip Hefner in the March 1977 issue of *Zygon: Journal of Religion and Science*.

8. Also see Burhoe 1966b, where he first formulates this interpretation, or translation, of the concept *supernatural*.

9. Burhoe found the key for solving this set of problems in a paper by J. Bronowski (1970).

10. I must note here that, in saying this, I have extrapolated the implication of Burhoe's hypothesis in the context of his thought. That God makes a difference is a controlling belief for Burhoe, grounded in his faith in the "Lord of History." Scientifically, Burhoe makes the more modest claim that religion plays the significant role in bonding the human gene pool and an independently selected culturetype in a mutually symbiotic relationship, with the human organism as the locus of this symbiosis. The human brain is the operational locus of the coadapted information in gene pool and culturetype. In the brain, these two sources of information are integrated to produce adaptive behaviors to meet the requirements of the environment for viability. Natural selection of behavior over time produces the mutual coadaptation of the two sources of information to the requirements of the larger environment. Religion has played an essential role in this process of coadaptation, without which humans could not have become sufficiently altruistic (beyond close kin) to have become civilized into cooperating, large social units of genetically unrelated individuals. I also point out that Burhoe himself differs with the more hard-line sociobiologists, represented by E. O. Wilson. For Wilson, culture is determined by epigenetic rules rooted in the rules that govern the natural selective mechanisms of a gene pool. For Burhoe, culture is a separate "species" from biological *Homo sapiens,* and the natural selective mechanisms in cultural systems are different from those that operate on the genetic systems.

REFERENCES

Aristotle. 1941. *Metaphysics* vi.1.1026ᵇ25. In *The Basic Works of Aristotle,* ed. Richard McKeon. New York: Random House.

Breed, David R. 1990. "Ralph Wendell Burhoe: His Life and His Thought: II. Formulating the Vision and Organizing the Institute on Religion in an Age of Science (IRAS)." *Zygon: Journal of Religion and Science* 25: 469-91.

⸻. 1991. "Ralph Wendell Burhoe: His Life and His Thought: III. Developing the Vision among the Unitarians, 1954-1964." *Zygon: Journal of Religion and Science* 26: 141-67.

Bronowski, J. 1970. "New Concepts in the Evolution of Complexity: Stratified Stability and Unbounded Plans." *Zygon: Journal of Religion and Science* 5: 18-35. Paper presented to the American Association for the Advancement of Science, Boston, 27 December 1969.

Burhoe, Ralph Wendell. 1963. "New Knowledge on the Nature of Moral and Mystical Experience." Paper presented at a conference on "Technological Change and Human Values," sponsored by the Center for Continuing Liberal Education at Pennsylvania State University, 4-6 December. Typescript.

⸻. 1964a. "The Lord of the Cosmos." Paper presented at a colloquy on "The Metaphysics of Physics: Theology and Physical Theory," Meadville Theological School, 13-14 January. Typescript.

⸻. 1964b. "The Lord of Mankind," in two parts: "Source and Sustainer of Man" and "Image of God or Soul." Papers presented at a colloquy on "The Metaphysics of Physics: Theology and Physical Theory," Meadville Theological School, 13-14 January. Typescript.

———. 1964c. "The Sciences, Humanities, and Religion—Can the Three Cultures Be Reunited?" Paper presented at the President's Annual Faculty Conference of St. Louis University on the general theme, "The Liberal Component of Undergraduate Education at St. Louis University," Pere Marquette State Park Lodge, Grafton, Ill., 11 September. Typescript.

———. 1964d. "A Theological Autobiography." Paper for the Faculty Seminar, Meadville Theological School, 6 November.

———. 1965. "Science and Liberal Religion." Paper presented at a conference on "Liberal Religion and the Sciences," the Unitarian Universalist Lake Geneva Summer Assembly, Lake Geneva, Wis., 4–10 July.

———. 1966a. "The Impact of Technology and the Sciences on Human Values: What Will Man Seek When All That He Values Is His by Automation?—The Dreams of Joseph and Jacob." In *Automation, Education and Human Values*, William Brickman and Stanley Lehrer. New York: School and Society Books. Paper presented to the seminar on "Work, Leisure, and Education in a Changing Industrialized Democracy," Center for Continuing Education, Pennsylvania State University, State College, Pa., 3–5 June, 1964.

———. 1966b. "Commentary on Theological Resources from the Social Sciences." *Zygon: Journal of Religion and Science* 1: 93–96.

———. 1966c. "Scientific Cosmos and Sacred Theos." In "Sketches of a Theological Structure Developed in the Light of the Sciences." Papers prepared for the Faculty Seminar, Meadville Theological School. Mimeo.

———. 1967. "Five Steps in the Evolution of Man's Knowledge of Good and Evil." *Zygon: Journal of Religion and Science* 2: 77–95. Paper presented at the 1965 IRAS Star Island Summer Conference.

———. 1969. "Theology and the Sciences at Meadville." Chicago: Burhoe Archives, 21 September. Mimeo.

———. 1972. "Natural Selection and God." *Zygon: Journal of Religion and Science* 7 (March): 30–63. Paper presented to the CASTS seminar, 27 April 1970.

———. 1973. "The Concepts of 'God' and 'Soul' in a Scientific View of Human Purpose." *Zygon: Journal of Religion and Science* 8 (December): 412–42. Paper presented at the Symposium on Science and Human Purpose, IRAS, Rensselaerville, N.Y., 25–30 October 1972.

———. 1975. "The Coming of Scientific Theology and Religious Revitalization." Paper presented in the symposium, "Prospects for Religion in the Next Quarter Century," Second General Assembly of the World Future Society, Washington, D.C., 2–5 June.

———. 1977. "What Does Determine Human Destiny?—Science Applied to Interpret Religion." *Zygon: Journal of Religion and Science* 12 (December): 336–89.

———. 1979. "Religion's Role in Human Evolution: The Missing Link between Ape-Man's Selfish Genes and Civilized Altruism." *Zygon: Journal of Religion and Science* 14 (June): 135–62. Paper presented to the Sociobiology Symposium. American Psychological Association, Toronto, 29 August 1978.

———. 1981. *Toward a Scientific Theology*. Dublin: Christian Journals.

———. 1984. "Cosmic Evolutionary Creation and Christian God." In *Cry of the Environment: Rebuilding the Christian Creation Tradition.*, ed. Philip W. Joranson and Ken Butigan, 218–52. Santa Fe: Bear & Company.

Burtt, Edwin Arthur. 1957. *The Metaphysical Foundations of Modern Physical Science*. Rev ed. New York: Doubleday.

Capek, Milec. 1961. *The Philosophical Impact of Contemporary Physics*. New York: D. Van Nostrand.

Chaisson, Eric J. 1979. "Cosmic Evolution: A Synthesis of Matter and Life." *Zygon: Journal of Religion and Science* 14 (March): 23–39.

Collingwood, R. G. 1945. *The Idea of Nature*. Oxford: Clarendon Press.

Frank, Philipp. 1957. *Philosophy of Science: The Link between Science and Philosophy*. Englewood Cliffs, N. J.: Prentice-Hall.

Koyre, Alexandre. 1957. *From the Closed World to the Infinite Universe*. New York: Harper & Row.

Lakatos, Imre. 1978. *The Methodology of Scientific Research Programmes*. Philosophical Papers, ed. John Worrall and Gregory Currie, vol. 1. Cambridge: Cambridge Univ. Press.

Meland, Bernard. 1967. "For the Modern Liberal: Is Theology Possible? Can Science Replace It?" *Zygon: Journal of Religion and Science* 2 (June): 166–86.

Mises, Richard von. 1951. *Positivism: A Study in Human Understanding*. Cambridge: Harvard Univ. Press.

Mortensen, Viggo. 1985. "Beyond Restriction and Expansion: A Possible Model for Relating Science and Religion." Paper presented at the Science and Religion Symposium. Seventeenth International Congress of History of Science, University of California at Berkeley, August.

Peacocke, Arthur. 1979. *Creation and the World of Science*. Oxford: Clarendon Press.

Shapley, Harlow. 1963. *The View from a Distant Star*. New York: Basic Books.

Toulmin, Stephen. 1982. *The Return to Cosmology: Postmodern Science and the Theology of Nature*. Berkeley and Los Angeles: Univ. of California Press.

Toynbee, Arnold. 1956. *An Historian's Approach to Religion*. London: Oxford Univ. Press.

Tracy, David, and Nicholas Lash, eds. 1983. *Cosmology and Theology*. Concilium: Religion in the Eighties Series. Edinburgh: T. & T. Clark, and New York: Seabury Press.

V The Struggle to Establish the Vision as a New Paradigm

This installment completes the discussion of the development of Burhoe's vision for revitalizing religion in the light of the sciences. I have already discussed the events leading to Burhoe's acceptance of the chairmanship of a new interdisciplinary Committee on Theology and the Frontiers of Learning at Meadville. The committee had the responsibility for developing the theology and science component of the New Design for Theological Education. This included developing curriculum for the professional training of persons for the liberal ministry, organizing a center for advanced research to support and undergird the curriculum, and launching a publications program. Institutional support for Burhoe's vision fostered the beginning of a Center for Advanced Study of Theology and the Sciences (CASTS) and, in cooperation with IRAS, a new journal, *Zygon*.

In *Zygon*, the proposed publication program of IRAS, which had been abandoned in 1958, became a reality in the joint venture with Meadville. That school provided the necessary resources of personnel, office space, support services, and money to produce the journal. IRAS joined in financial support and provided a wide network of scholars and a source of papers from its conferences. The two institutions contracted to establish the journal through a Joint Publication Board. Representing Meadville were Sutherland, Hayward, and Tapp; representing IRAS were Sanborn Brown, Kirtley Mather, and Burhoe. The twenty-one members of the Editorial Advisory Board also served on the Scientific Advisory Board for CASTS. The services of the University of Chicago Press were secured to produce and distribute the journal, whose first issue was published in March 1966.

Beginning with the first editorial, Burhoe continued to articulate the guiding vision to keep the journal focused on the primary agenda: "imaginatively and informedly to structure theories or beliefs about man, the world, and man's hopes and duties thereunder, which integrate with our new heritage of valid knowledge and, at the same time, effectively operate to supply our religious needs'' (Burhoe 1966a, 9–10). With some assistance from Tapp, who was assigned by Meadville to be managing editor, Burhoe drafted the first editorial, which set out the presuppositions, goals, and policies for the journal. "I spent weeks polishing it on Little Whortleberry Island in Lake Winnepesaukee, N.H., during the summer of 1965. It was printed by the University of Chicago Press in the fall as our prospectus for the journal, and sent to a few hundred scientific, theological, and other colleagues to enlist support'' (Burhoe 1988). I quote in full the first section, because, as Karl Peters, who succeeded Burhoe as editor in 1979, has said, "these paragraphs give a clear picture of the territory that *Zygon* and its sponsoring organizations are trying to map'' (Peters 1987, 44).

Zygon, the Greek term for anything which joins two bodies, especially the yoking or harnessing of a team which must effectively pull together, is a symbol for this journal whose aim is to reunite the split team, values and knowledge, where coordination is essential for a viable dynamics of human culture.

We respond to the growing fears that the widening chasm in twentieth-century culture between values and knowledge, or good and truth, or religion and science, is disruptive if not lethal for human destiny. In this split, the traditional faiths and philosophies, which once informed men of what is of most sacred concern for them, have lost their credibility and hence their power. Yet human fulfillment or salvation in the age of science requires not less but more insight and conviction concerning life's basic values.

Zygon has rich connotations in the sciences, where it supplies the biological term "zygote," designating the union of two gametes or complementary halves of the genetic code essential for the continuation and advancement of life. Here we have the image of two sets of different blueprints for life, each from an ancient lineage. And it is only by their effective yoking that a new generation or a more effective pattern of life can emerge. At the same time, *zygon* has symbolized in religion the union between man and the ultimate reality on which his life depends, as in the Christian "for my yoke [*zygos* in the Greek New Testament] is easy [or good]," or as in the Sanskrit and Hindu cognate *yoga*, meaning union of self with the universal reality.

Ordinarily, in the evolution of human cultures, beliefs and practices about man's most sacred concerns necessarily have been integrated with the concurrent general beliefs and practices—the sciences (philosophies, world views, myths) and technologies. Disruption by historical changes of this integration between basic values and science, or between sacred and secular knowledge, automatically brings about pressures for new adaptations of one or the other or both to reintegrate the organization of the culture. Failure to reintegrate satisfactorily has spelled the death of cultures or civilizations.

One might say that because of its radical mutations the cultural "gamete" from father science has not yet found any corresponding gamete from mother religion with which it can unite to form a workable new culture for future civilization. A valid union may require mutations or reformations in religious belief systems, or further mutations in scientific belief systems, or both. The journal *Zygon* is established as a workshop for those seeking ways to unite, in full integrity, the sciences with what men hold to be their sacred values, their religion (Burhoe 1966a, 1–2).

In his editorials and articles, Burhoe sought to give coherence to the workshop by relating articles by others to the central aims and vision of the journal which were also his own. In the March 1968 issue, Burhoe said that it was time to evaluate the course of the expedition "to reach religion by using the sciences." He pointed out three motivational weaknesses: lack of a clear vision of why religion is necessary to structure and transmit fundamental values, lack of a coherent scientific picture of man and his world yet to be constructed out of the scattered pieces of an unfinished jigsaw puzzle, and lack of sufficient attention to the central religious problems.

We should focus on assembling first those jigsaw-puzzle pieces that look most promising for giving us an overarching sketch of the nature and source of man's central values, duties, hopes, and destiny—the modern equivalent of the central values found in the great religious myths or theologies of the past two or three thousand years. . . . An overarching and religiously relevant vision logically depends on formulations of man's ultimate destiny as far as we can envision it and on what is required of him if he is to have hope for his fulfillment or salvation in the context of the reality upon which he believes he is in the end dependent. . . . If we could agree more clearly on what the source and determiner of destiny is, I think we could then begin to make more rapid progress in reaching our goal of a scientifically grounded religion (Burhoe 1968, 4–5).

Here he made clear the theological ramifications and orientation of the agenda for *Zygon* and its importance for revitalizing religion.

The theological agenda of the journal and Burhoe's leadership did not go unnoticed. Patrick Milburn, in a review of *Zygon,* wrote,

Born of an intense awareness of the cultural crisis of the Western world, particularly as it manifests itself in relation to our Judeo-Christian heritage, *Zygon* has sought to illumine the basic issues which relate theology to the natural and anthropological sciences, and more recently has begun to lay the foundations of a creative, contextual theology for an ethics of the human environment (Milburn 1971, 71–72).

Its weaknesses notwithstanding, he said that *Zygon* was a deeply valuable effort which has been treating some of the most fundamental and exciting issues confronting our contemporary cultural life. The weaknesses Milburn identified related to suggestive directions which had not been explored. In spite of Northrop's suggestive remark that radical immediacy does not warrant belief in a substance of any kind (Northrop 1966, 37) and the amount of attention paid to evolution, he said that in *Zygon* he found the adoption of a substance cosmology with the emphasis on transformation. He did not find that problems with the tautological character of the concept of selection had been explored, especially in the light of work indicating the great potential of individual organisms as agents in the process of evolution. "*Zygon* has presented excellent reviews of present orthodoxy, without engaging in essential criticism." The enterprise was limited in that "there is no effort to envision or evoke the form that mythological thought may take in our time, no efforts like those of Ricoeur or Elizabeth Sewell to engage the mythic as a creative form of thought." He said that IRAS did not seem intent on identifying the kinds of intellectual syntheses that might expose or evoke the symbolic unities, as well as the conceptual principles, which give meaning to human life.

Out of a great toleration, no position has yet emerged which correlates the natural and social sciences with an effective ethics grounded in a renewed theology. . . . Some of the essays seem to suggest great possibilities for a creative new theology that could take into account current epistemological and ethical questions, and relate these to fertile elements in Judeo-Christian heritage.

This review appeared during a time of creative chaos. Meadville was having to cut back its support for CASTS as well as the journal; CASTS was mutating into CASIRAS; and the viability of *Zygon* was in question for lack of funds. In the March 1972 issue Burhoe pointed out important contributions which helped to sustain the journal for seven years. He singled out Fowler McCormick, president and chairman of the board of International Harvester Company, to symbolize "our debt to many members of IRAS who have given wisdom to the editor as well as money to its *Zygon* fund . . . that has been necessary for the life of the journal." He acknowledged the generous support of Meadville which "made possible the Center and helped bring *Zygon* into being." And he acknowledged the cooperation of the University of Chicago Press and the concern and wisdom of editorial advisers and helpers. However, the journal was in need of a broader base of support so that it might become self-sustaining. "We need help in finding more such people who are ready to wrestle with the difficult problems of attempting to unify our religious understanding with contemporary scientific knowledge so that religion can be more effective in its salvatory function in an age of science." In reference to Milburn's review, he noted that "we have not yet adequately succeeded in fulfilling our aim to provide a genuine unification, yoking, or *zygon* of religion and science." Burhoe concurred with Milburn that humanity's greatest hope and opportunity lie in the development of a creative new theology, although for Burhoe that new theology must extend beyond the Judeo-Christian to the other great religious heritages. He noted that to provide more of the element Milburn was commending, a number of advisers had urged him to publish more of his own papers. Responding to their advice, "beginning about a year ago I have put into *Zygon* several of my papers, hoping thereby to show how the various sciences may be seen to relate to one another and to traditional theology in a coherent or unified view of human destiny" (Burhoe 1972a, 2–5).

Because of the amount of his own writing in the journal, some have perceived *Zygon* as Burhoe's journal. While there is some truth in this, it nonetheless is largely mistaken. Although Burhoe's philosophy guided the journal, he maintained a commitment to scholarly impeccability through the editorial advisory board, which referred submissions, including his own. Burhoe did not operate alone, but only with the concurrence of advisers and the Joint Publications Board. Although these advisers did not necessarily fully agree with Burhoe's perspective, they did see his thought as representative of the kind of synthesis sought by the *Zygon* community. On his part, Burhoe was the only one bold enough to claim that, for the most part, his developing perspective attempted to represent the synthesis of the tradition of thought exemplified in *Zygon:*

I am suggesting that the new views held by a number of us associated with the development of *Zygon* represent a new paradigm, a new perspective for looking upon both religious and scientific "truth," that brings both sets of "truth" into a common system (Burhoe 1977, 339).

Because I have found no evidence to the contrary, I do not believe it can be shown that Burhoe was merely promoting his own personal philosophy. Rather, I have concluded that Burhoe was promoting a personal philosophy which he held in common with a significant number of respected scientists, philosophers, and religious scholars. To make the point more strongly, I suggest that if Burhoe had become aware that his personal involvement and writing stood in the way of advancing the program of the new paradigm, he would have dropped out of public view for the sake of that program. As nearly as I can discern, that never was the case. It should be evident from all that has been said that, in spite of differences of opinion, there was support in the *Zygon* community for the general direction of Burhoe's attempted synthesis.[1]

Burhoe encouraged, published, and responded to criticisms of the *Zygon* hypothesis:[2]

In today's culture, where the greatest aura of factuality is possessed by scientific models of what is true, religious myths or theologies may find a new resource for interpreting the invisible realities. The program set forth as the basis for *Zygon* is to provide translations between the truths latent in traditional religious symbol systems and the scientific symbol systems, thus to restore a genuine aura of factuality (Burhoe 1974, 5).

Although he encouraged critical perspectives, the journal met with difficulties from the University of Chicago Press. Sutherland summed up the problem in his reflections:

The story of the interplay of individuals and ideologies who began to wrestle for control of the journal is too long to record here, but when it became clear to the University Divinity School that the Publications Board supported Burhoe's editorial policy and expected to retain Burhoe as editor, the Press became restless and the need to find a new "home" for *Zygon* became clear (Sutherland 1987, 24).

This was at a time in which the journal was in a somewhat weakened position. Burhoe had retired from Meadville in 1974, and CASIRAS, although affiliated with the Chicago Cluster of Theological Schools (and with office space given by the Lutheran School of Theology), had not been funded to support an editorial office to replace the resources given by Meadville through 1974. The editing and production of the journal was in large part the result of volunteer efforts, not the least of which was Burhoe's. In 1975 the editorial team was expanded with four associate editors: Sanborn Brown, Don Browning, Philip Hefner, and Solomon Katz (Burhoe 1975b, 10–11). In addition to limited funds, in 1976 and 1977 Burhoe's failing health (including coronary bypass surgery), contributed to the journal's falling behind in its production schedule.

The situation, which produced a spate of activity and discussion within IRAS and CASIRAS, opened for reexamination the purposes of those organizations and their relationship to *Zygon*. Burhoe vigorously engaged in discussion, encouraging the reexamination, and continued to hold up the vision of the enterprise in terms of the original charters and history. Offers came from the Boston Theological Institute, the Lutheran School of Theology, and Rollins College. One of the deciding factors in the final decision to accept the offer from Rollins College was the need for a new and younger editor to carry on the policies of *Zygon*. Karl Peters, who surfaced as the person most available for the task, had the newfound support and interest of Rollins College in carrying on the *Zygon* project. By the middle of 1979 the transition to a new home for *Zygon* had been accomplished. In brief, the outcome of the reexamination was the affirmation of new leadership for *Zygon,* a renewed vision for IRAS, and a confirmation and rededication of support among the members of CASIRAS.

In his last editorial as editor, Burhoe wrote,

Zygon is a community venture, a community and a venture which it has been my privilege to have served for more than three decades. The community includes all those who have been listed on its editorial board over the years, most of the authors it has published, and a considerable population of conference arrangers and participants. This community has been important for *Zygon* since it has had to generate most of the relevant papers as well as judge their worth in this program for developing a new paradigm for understanding the relation of values and facts (Burhoe 1978, 251).

The community behind the publication of *Zygon* has opted for interpreting religion in the light of the sciences, the path chosen by Teilhard, although our community began . . . before we knew of Teilhard and has not followed his particular interpretations except by coincidence. We have been an independent group of persons who have sought to be fully scientific and at the same time seriously concerned to understand and if possible to revitalize the religious- and morality-generating institutions of society with the help of scientific interpretation of our need for their function and their truth (Burhoe 1979a, 4).

In his reflections on *Zygon* and the Center, Sutherland said,

That journal, Ralph [Burhoe] has suggested, is perhaps the most significant tangible contribution the Center has made, and his editorship kept its mission clear and explicit, and consequently saved it from becoming a journal for papers generally in the field of religion and science and more explicitly for papers which might contribute to or challenge the discovery and enrichment of scientifically justified theological affirmations (Sutherland 1987, 24).

Apart from his other writings, *Zygon* is certainly Burhoe's most important work and major contribution to the intellectual grappling with the many problems in adapting traditional religious wisdom to the religious and spiritual needs of persons in an age of science and technology.

THE CENTER FOR ADVANCED STUDY

At the same time that *Zygon* was gaining stature, Burhoe was nurturing the program of the Center for Advanced Study in Theology and the Sciences (CASTS). From the beginning, he had argued that its ideas were too immature and untested for introduction into professional education and needed to be developed in a research center. Thus the Center was an essential component of the New Design and considered fundamental to the effectiveness of the Committee. In addition to research and writing to support and undergird the theological curriculum, the Center was to guide advanced- and post-degree scholars, to conduct programs of continuing education, and to have a publications program (Meadville Theological School 1964, 11). It was the promise of developing such a Center for advanced study, of extending the work he had been doing in his spare time with some members of the Academy (in IRAS and the UUA Commission), that had lured Burhoe to accept leadership for the Meadville project. Sutherland and the Board heartily supported the Center and Burhoe's vision for it, even at a significant financial risk. They committed funds for fellowships to stimulate formation of a critical mass of scholars and for a scholarly publication to disseminate the fruits of research for criticism and utilization by a broader world of scholarship. Burhoe's vision was the guiding light for the Center, as a 1966 announcement of postdoctoral fellowships shows:

This non-sectarian Center was established in 1964 . . . to encourage an open, imaginative, and informed interacting community of theologians, scientists, and other scholars concerned with examining religious practices, ethical values, and theological concepts in the light of contemporary science. The Center's task is one of reinterpretation and innovation: reinterpretation of the heritage of religion in keeping with the reality picture of the sciences; innovation in religious method and content to meet the demands of a new age. The Center also includes in its task a continuing assessment of the negative and positive influences of technology and cybernation upon human beings and their value systems today. The ultimate aim is a renaissance of religious synthesis.

Burhoe's developing program for a scientific theology was offered as a paradigmatic option for critical discussion when he presented his "Sketches" in the first advanced seminar in the winter of 1966. As it had in IRAS, his programmatic vision served as the heuristic hub of the Center, giving direction and focus to its program. As noted, one primary requirement was a critical mass of competent scholars and advanced students committed to developing the field. To achieve this and to seek guidance for establishing the Center was the purpose of a proposal for "A One-year Trial Balloon" grant whose opening sentence capsulized Burhoe's vision for the Center: "On scientific and rational as well as intuitive and emotional grounds there is a strong case for the necessity of credible religious beliefs to give structure and direction to individual attitudes and social behavior if any society of men is to be viable" (Burhoe 1965).

Burhoe proposed that twelve fellows, mostly young scholars with some distinction, be selected for one year of work from 1966 to 1967. In the summer of 1966 some twenty distinguished and creative scholars who had made contributions to the field (most of those on the Scientific Advisory Board) would gather with the director and other fellows for a five-week period to chart the course of fruitful research for the coming year. The following summer the group would convene again for a five-week period of evaluation and setting of future goals and program for the Center. Funding was not forthcoming for such an ambitious program, however, the Board provided funds for some fellowships, secretarial services, and *Zygon,* and made office and seminar space available for Center operations to begin in fall of 1966.

For three years (1966 to 1969) the Center functioned on a small scale with only a handful of full-time resident fellows in addition to Burhoe and occasional visiting scholars. Burhoe was gifted at providing a comfortable, congenial working atmosphere, and there were regular weekly seminars (on Fridays) and occasional "extraordinary" seminars. The Center staff, joined by other faculty members and students in an informal "peripatetic college," attended nearby lectures, meetings, and conferences. Kenneth Cauthen, the first postdoctoral fellow, spent a sabbatical year at the Center working on a book which "elaborates an experimental, tentative perspective on nature, history, man, and God designed to fit the present cultural situation" (Cauthen 1969, 9).

In the winter of 1966, Cauthen was joined by Henry Nelson Wieman, and in spring they were joined by John Ruskin Clark, the first research associate. Clark was given sabbatical by his congregation to work on a book "written in response to the hunger in our society for meaningful and viable religion" (Clark 1977, ix). In 1967 and 1968 there were two postdoctoral fellows. George Riggan, professor of systematic theology at the Hartford Seminary Foundation, took a sabbatical year to study the scientific aspects of the work of Teilhard de Chardin, which was just becoming available (Riggan 1968). He was joined by Donald R. Gentner, who had just finished a Ph.D. in chemistry at Berkeley and now took the opportunity to explore theology and science (Gentner 1968, 432–41).

Administering the Center, Burhoe was in the same role he had served so effectively at Blue Hill and then at the American Academy. His graciousness and great rapport with scientists and scholars contributed to his building of an interdisciplinary community in religion and science. Moreover, his orientation to advanced research (one of the primary reasons he had been brought to Meadville) was also a great strength. He could envision how various forms of research might contribute to the field, and he encouraged persons to explore the relation of their work to religious issues in the seminars of the Center.

In February 1967 the Center began a cooperative effort, with the UUA Department of Education, to develop a third- and fourth-grade curriculum, which in 1971 was published as part of the new Beacon curriculum under the title "*Our Human Heritage.*" From 1968 to 1971 Burhoe and John Godbey participated in the six meetings of an ad hoc group of Midwestern Unitarian Universalist scientists and theologians, called the "Colloquium on Man." Pittsburgh Theological Seminary sought Burhoe's help in organizing a symposium on science and values as part of its 175th anniversary celebration in March 1970. In April 1970 Burhoe attended a meeting of representatives of some thirty-nine institutes and associations concerned about the relationship between theology and the sciences and technology. The meeting resulted in a permanent international secretariat of a seven-person clearinghouse for information and for monitoring further developments (Burhoe 1970a).

In 1968 the retirement of Hayward prompted an evaluation and planning process to decide how to use resources thus released. In the course of that process it became clear that Meadville could no longer give sufficient financial support to sustain the activities of the Center. Riggan joined Sutherland, Donald Harrington (a member of the Board of Trustees), Burhoe, and others in a prolonged evaluation of the Center (Riggan 1987, 31). In 1969, because of increasing financial problems, Meadville suspended support for postdoctoral fellowships. Alternatives were explored, including working with the University of Chicago Divinity School and the Chicago Cluster of Theological Schools (CCTS) in Hyde Park. There was interest in the work of the Center among a number of scientists and theologians who, though not associated with Meadville, participated in its seminars and other programs.

MUTATION OF CASTS INTO CASIRAS

In the summer of 1970 (four years after *Zygon* first appeared), Burhoe engaged Riggan and Cauthen in extensive discussions to draft a proposal for reconstituting CASTS, to appeal more broadly for financial support as well as attracting staff and students. Of particular note was their concern that the expression "theology and the sciences" was a hindrance in communication. "Life values," "human values," and "human destiny" were among the substitutes entertained for the word *theology* (*human destiny* was preferred because of its futuristic orientation). In February 1971 Burhoe wrote the proposal on the future of the Center, which recommended the expansion of CASTS to offer advanced degree work for the D.Min. and Ph.D. (Burhoe 1971a). It noted the necessity to broaden the base of the Center beyond that of a parochial UU agency in order to attract financial resources, students, and the cooperation of faculty at other schools. It was presented to the Long-Range Planning Committee of the Board of Trustees, which recommended that Burhoe and Sutherland explore ways to implement it.

The outcome, at a meeting at Community Church in New York City on 5 March 1972, was the official founding of the Center for Advanced Study in Religion and Science to replace CASTS. The central aim of CASIRAS was "to formulate a specific and coherent system of belief about human destiny, a 'doctrine of human destiny' which has the necessary credibility to motivate men generally toward a new level of faith and responsibility in the coming world society'' (Burhoe 1972d, 172). To accomplish this,

the Center would seek to bind together in a more or less loosely knit collegium a significant number of those still rather rare and widely scattered scholars and creative minds in various disciplines who have already shown interest in and capacity for constructive integration of the functions and beliefs of religion with the beliefs of the contemporary sciences. . . . CASIRAS might be called an ''Invisible College for the Development of Religious Thought in the Light of the Sciences'' (Burhoe 1972d, 178).

At its annual meeting in the summer of 1972, IRAS resolved to accept CASIRAS, which was to assume the previous responsibilities of CASTS, as the copublisher of *Zygon,* and it also resolved to expand its membership. Burhoe identified the partnership of IRAS and CASIRAS as that between a membership organization and a center for research and teaching (Burhoe 1973a, 70–71). In October, the second symposium of the IRAS Committee on Science and Human Values was held at the Institute on Man and Science in Rensselaer-ville, New York, on the theme ''Science and Human Purpose.'' In part, this symposium explored the possibility of relocating the Center, or at least its proposed summer programs, in Rensselaerville. The State University of New York (SUNY) at Albany was another institution excited by the prospect of relocating CASIRAS and establishing a doctoral program in Religion and Science. It too was enthusiastic in their invitation. Burhoe, Riggan, Sutherland and others explored the possibility with considerable care. On 5 February 1973 CASIRAS was fully incorporated in New York as a not-for-profit institution ''to study the relationship between religion and science with a view towards integrating religious beliefs and values with the conceptual systems of contemporary science.'' In September 1973 a grant proposal ''for Developing New Moral and Ethical Frameworks,'' developed in cooperation with the Boston Theological Institute, was submitted to the Rockefeller Foundation. It was hoped that this grant would provide CASIRAS with the funds needed for a five-year program, but the grant was not forthcoming.

In June 1974, the following year, after Burhoe retired from Meadville, CASIRAS and *Zygon* were given office space by the Lutheran School of Theology at Chicago (LSTC). CASIRAS became affiliated with the Chicago Cluster of Theological Schools (CCTS), superseded by the Association of Chicago Theological Schools (ACTS). CASIRAS offered a regular advanced seminar and an occasional M.Div. course. In 1976, with the support of CASIRAS, LSTC included a theology and science specialization in its doctoral program in the theological area. By then, Sutherland and Tapp had left

Meadville, thus closing the books on a decade-long effort to incorporate the theology and science area into the regular program at Meadville as part of the New Design for theological education.

GRIEF AND REJOICING: A MARRIAGE ENDS, ANOTHER BEGINS

In 1967 Burhoe's wife, Frances, who suffered from glial cancer, died in August. Burhoe wrote and published a personal account of her contribution to his life and work and to the larger community, concluding:

> She lived very close to her husband in family and fun, in vocation and avocation. She encouraged him in his wild dreams, which were often ridiculous to others. Four years ago, she encouraged him, even persuaded him, to go to Chicago on another strange adventure to relate religion to the sciences. The pair were knit together tightly by many common bonds, and the pain of separation is terrible.
>
> Our loss of an immediate, personal presence is great; but our gain is great in terms of the continuing manifestations of the crystal jewels, which have spun off from the eddy of atoms that was she, and live within and among us in the larger, ongoing stream of life.
>
> The vision that life begins at birth and ends at death of the body is myopic illusion. The vision that our ultimate concerns and values are confined to this temporal sack of blood and bones is equally short-sighted and the source of tragedy. We humans have to learn anew in the verbally transmitted patterns of our culture what our animal ancestors knew in their genes: that the ultimate values and reality of our life far transcend the brief hour and the small sack that struts upon this stage.
>
> No man is an island, either in the dimension of space or time. The full meaning of life can come to us only when we recognize as the true soul and value of our being, not merely that temporary and only seemingly separate atomic eddy, but more fully and ultimately that larger, immortally advancing pattern, integrated by real and unbreakable ties with the depth, breadth, and length of the stream of life and its cosmic source.
>
> This is at once a scientific and a religious truth. We have not heretofore been clearly enough aware of it, for, without this truth ingrained in both mind and heart, rational men find it difficult either to deal with death or to love their fellow men as themselves (Burhoe 1967).

On Easter Sunday, 6 April 1969, Burhoe married recently widowed Calla Butler. The Burhoes and the Butlers had enjoyed earlier associations at Arlington Street Church in Boston and through work with the UUA. Dana Greeley wrote of their meeting and marriage:

> The open house on New Year's Day [1969] was attended by two old friends at Arlington Street Church, each now left alone because of the death of the partner. Calla Butler was then working in my office, and Ralph Burhoe happened to drop in from Chicago. They met most pleasantly, and I married them on Easter. The wedding would have been at 25 Beacon Street, but Robert Hohler's

sit-in against the UUA's investment policies was in full swing at that moment and a substantial attraction and encumbrance at headquarters. . . . [We] went down the hill to King's Chapel for the wedding in the Little Chapel. It was a lovely wedding for two wonderful people, now very much a part of the Meadville family but always of the denominational family as well (Greeley 1971, 75).

Calla gave gracious and energetic support to Burhoe's work, as well as the work of the Center, during a marriage of more than twenty years that encompassed some of Burhoe's most productive periods.

A DEVELOPING INTELLECTUAL STRUCTURE

The sixteen years following Burhoe's arrival in Chicago—the period 1964 to 1980—were extremely productive. He was sought out for his perspective on the relation of religion and science and for his organizational and promotional abilities. He was involved in organizing conferences, editing *Zygon*, lecturing, and continuing his own research and writing. He also devoted time and energy to promoting a scientific approach to religious problems and to elaborating his own research program for developing a scientific theology.

Burhoe's agenda was to promote religious enlightenment through a rational interpretation of religion in the light of the sciences— that is, a scientific theology. As the rise of the modern sciences has enlightened the human mind to the intricate workings of the natural world and thereby opened new vistas of technological exploitation of the new knowledge thus revealed, so too, he thought, the sciences can enlighten the human mind to comprehend the essential role of religion for human welfare.

Theology is the attempt to interpret the religious heritage in the most universal and valid forms of rational discourse, which for me and increasing others are the sciences. I find scientific interpretation capable of revitalizing the wisdom hidden in earlier theologies, myths, and mores by making them newly credible. . . .

On the grounds of my approach to theology in the light of the sciences, I feel confident that there will be a revitalization of religion, a religion operative among all peoples and cultures . . . , a religion that is as credible as atoms and gravity, a religion which will harmonize the ideas and behaviors in the various cultures and populations of the world, and enable them to adapt viably to life in a worldwide and transworld community dominated by fantastic evolutionary transformations of genes and cultures (Burhoe 1982b).

During this period, Burhoe worked hard to persuade others of the importance of this agenda.

Again, Burhoe sought to synthesize and integrate into his developing scientific theology the essential issues and results of ongoing discussions of what he called "an invisible college for the study of values and religion." Burhoe's writing, including his published pieces, was done in response to requests—proposals and reports, papers for conferences and seminars, summaries of conferences, topical rationales and questions for focusing a conference or seminar. A few, however, were written for a collection of articles on a specific topic which did not result from a conference (Burhoe 1973b, 1982b, 1984b).

The Structure of Burhoe's Theology. In a paper sketching the rationale for the work of the Scientific Advisory Board for CASTS, Burhoe presented the following argument. "While the dominant views of the past century have held that religion is a division of culture inherently divorced from that of the sciences, there have been some who hold that he who has found science in opposition to religion has never properly understood either" (Burhoe 1970d, 110). If religions were understood in terms of the basic invariant functions or needs they serve, instead of the culturally relative practices or ideologies in which they are manifested, "the sciences may be as useful for advancing religious theory and for improving religious practice (concerned with the general salvation of man) as they are for medical theory and practice (concerned with human salvation limited primarily to general organic problems)" (Burhoe 1970d, 111).

From an evolutionary perspective, religion can be seen as one among the arts of human culture whose evolution can be described as accumulations of know-how and wisdom, selected, without human design or plan, from among numerous accidental or chance cultural modifications of the genetically based biological systems for maintaining life, by the genetically established conditioned mechanisms of individuals in societies for the relative viability or fitness they bestowed. If we conceive of a logical hierarchy of values, at the peak of which is the most invariant and ultimate value—life—and this hierarchy could be objectively demonstrated, then the religious area would be differentiated in its reality from other areas as that concerned with the adaptiveness of the organism to the ultimate requirements of life. Thus "ideally, and probably to a large extent in fact in history, all the other social institutions and their characteristic arts or technologies may be said to be integrated into the service of the general goals or values set by the religions" (Burhoe 1970d, 117).

Having defined religion as an evolving cultural art whose function is to orient us to the ultimate goals and conditions for life at the top of the hierarchy of values, he said: "Our problem now is: In the light of the new scientific images of the nature of man and the total reality upon which he is dependent, what can be the overarching doctrines for resolving his ultimate concerns?'' (Burhoe 1964, 6). Or later, formulated in more scientific terms, ''What are or should be the overarching values that order his ultimate concerns?'' (Burhoe 1970d, 118). He went on to say that ''our primary task is to build a new community of minds in which the new knowledge or information about facts in general is directly connected with the basic facts about life's values'' (Burhoe 1970d, 119). Commenting on method, he wrote:

> I do not view the general method of research in this approach to religious or theological problems through the sciences as being primarily a matter of employing the scientific method at the empirical, testing level to develop new science, at least not for the near future. It would seem more fruitful to consider our problem as one of applying the already scientifically validated conceptual models of "reality" . . . to the problems of religion. In this sense, religious science (theology), like medical science, would be primarily an area of applied science. . . .
>
> The solutions to religious problems . . . are, like solutions to problems of medical health, partially supplied by the following three sources of wisdom: genotypic, organic, and anciently evolved cultural formulas. A fourth source is applied science. . . . I suspect that man's capacity to survive depends on his success in finding a new, rational, and scientific illumination and ordering of these religious problems. . . . It is my belief that the wealth of information in the contemporary sciences . . . offers the best hope to those who would seek viable answers to these problems of man's ultimate concerns or values (Burhoe 1970d, 120–21).

Values. In a number of papers Burhoe elaborated his ontology, epistemology, and axiology in order to make the case that science can study values, that science is the best source of new revelations of the sacred truth about values, that science could provide the basis for a worldwide consensus on values, and that the primary sources for his theology were the sciences, organized to interpret religion and addressed to religious questions. In 1967 he published an exposition of his evolutionary theory of knowledge ''to make what seems to me a coherent picture of man's long history of learning to distinguish good from evil.'' At the end of the paper he concluded that the sciences as the sources of valid information and new revelations were the best hope for finding a renewed authority for values. On another occasion he argued that religious symbolic systems and institutions are the traditional cultural agencies for storing and transmitting evolving sacred goals. Because those symbol systems have not incorporated the new conceptual language and information about values coming from the sciences, we are in danger of losing the essential information for life encoded in those symbols. What is needed is an effective new applied science which would integrate contemporary scientific concepts into a growing system of symbols concerning human goals and destiny (Burhoe 1966b).

In a number of papers he developed the idea that values are a class of facts, a kind of knowledge or information, which are intrinsic to the process of life and give the living agency the capacity to remain in being. Values are the norms and goals embodied in cybernetic mechanisms of living systems which function to maintain the dynamic homeostatic balance of a system in an ever-changing environment. In "Values via Science" he presented "a plausible outline of how the sciences do in fact reveal and make available to human consciousness much more detail about our human values, their origins, the cybernetic mechanisms (biological and cultural) in which they are encoded, their evolution, and even some visions of how new values may be evolved to transport us to transcend our present humanity." The reason for arguing that the sciences reveal values was given in the next sentence:

Our most urgent and immediate goal is that of the more rapid evolution of certain elements of our present cultural structures and their integration with the sciences, namely our present cultural programs for transmitting, reforming, and motivating values. . . . In our present ecological system, anything less than an enlightenment of our human values via the sciences portends only increasing chaos and self-destruction of man, and possibly the destruction of much if not all of the values inherent in other biological life (Burhoe 1969, 91–92).

That goal can be accomplished by showing that human values have their source and sanction in the total transhuman environment that has evoked and selected the evolving patterns of life.

Thermodynamics. In a paper by Bronowski (1970), Burhoe found a solution to the problem of connecting the worlds of physics and biology. "Bronowski, in his concept of 'stratified stability,' has at last given a neat physical formulation that underlies all levels of the selective or adaptive process in evolution from atoms to human cultural patterns." For Burhoe, it was a concept of nature which could provide "a generalized and physical model of how the natural selection process works at all levels" (Burhoe 1970c, 39–40). In "Natural Selection and God" he proposed that such a conception of natural selection, extended to cover the whole of cosmic evolution, including all phases of human evolution, was a way of describing the mighty acts of God in history. In this picture nature is sovereign and selects or judges the random, trial-and-error searches of its interacting elements to meet the requirements for stability inherent in nature itself. Progress in evolution is the exploration of adaptive possibilities driven by an entropic energy flow up the ladder of stratified stabilities to ever more complex but stable configurations (Burhoe 1972b, 30–63).

He reflected on a number of areas where he saw the gropings of the evolutionary process toward new levels of complexity, perhaps leading to some transhuman species as in the possible case of an emerging symbiosis of humans and computers (Burhoe 1972c). He considered simply mistaken the claims that humans are in control of their destiny. Whether in managing human behavior to promote environmental health (Burhoe 1972e) or in the development of new genetic technologies, it is the same nature which has selected and incarnated value in the evolutionary progression of living systems that will continue to select viable systems in the future (Burhoe 1971b). In world-system modeling he saw an attempt, similar to his own, to comprehend the system that ultimately determines human destiny. He suggested that a missing but crucial aspect was consideration of the ultimate human values evolved in religious traditions. He predicted that the motivation to establish widespread human behavior in accord with the long-range values needed to avert projected catastrophe would await the revitalization of religion. "This is not likely to take place until the wisdom already evolved within the traditions is translated and interpreted within today's more extended and credible views of man and the world developed by the sciences" (Burhoe 1973d, 182).

Evolution of Religion.   Burhoe thought he foresaw the evolution of religions in the chapters he contributed to *Science and Human Values in the 21st Century* (Burhoe 1971c). At the end of that book he prophesied that twenty-first–century values will come from a scientifically based theology that creates a common world culture:

I prophesy that each of the religions will tend to be resurrected or revitalized and transformed as it effectively translates the viable wisdom of its tradition into this new symbol system of the sciences, and as it reforms and extends the traditional wisdom to adapt human living to the requirements for living in the new one-world culture of increasingly closely interdependent billions of people on Spaceship Earth. . . . So long as the scientific-technological world view continues to spread, natural selection as it operates in cultural evolution is going to weed out the religions that are unfit for motivating men to ordered or viable behavior in that world (Burhoe 1971c, 184–85).

The cornerstone for human and all other values is the concept of God. That there is a God who selects and ordains human destiny has been a central message of the religions of the world, and this concept is confirmed in the scientific myths of a lawful cosmic evolution:

Every creature is constantly seeking new and better adjustments. The progress of life's development from molecules to men, and from infants to men, is the result of constant trials in search of what the Lord ordains. It is written in our very genes that we, who are in so large part graced with life because of what they program for us, must constantly seek to adapt ourselves in new and better ways to the requirements laid down by the larger nature or Lord for the further development or evolution of life. Those individuals and species of life who do not constantly seek to adapt to the sovereign requirements of what must be done to remain in being simply are among those who once were and no longer are (Burhoe 1971c, 198–99).

He concluded the book:

Human values are set by the natural Lord God Almighty, not by man. For man is a blade of grass that grows in the day and is gone by night, but the total system of reality or nature reigns forever. Man's privilege and man's only hope is to adapt, to serve the will of the Lord.

Such a vision is not novel except for the conviction with which it may be held in the twentieth century by one who finds it revealed in the scientific myth of creation. Such a vision may allow one to try to bring about a reformation of theology in the light of the sciences without total assurance that it will come in time, or that it will come at all.

Our task is forever to discern the will of the Most High and then seek to fulfill it, forever confessing our errors and reforming our ways (Burhoe 1971c, 202).

The Concept of Soul. Burhoe's paper, "The Concepts of God and Soul in a Scientific View of Human Purpose," for the Symposium on Science and Human Purpose in October 1972, marks a watershed in his research and writing. In that paper he said: "For understanding human purpose not only do we need a doctrine of the scheme of things that ultimately determines human destiny, but also we need to understand man as an element of that system" (Burhoe 1973c, 432). He argues that a concept of soul is necessary to provide the proper understandings and feelings to motivate individual humans in service of the purposes ordained for their evolution by God—the ultimate system that selects or determines destiny. In his subsequent papers he tended to focus more extensively on that which is essentially human. For example, he focused on the individual human in "The Nature of Man as a Niche in Nature and as an Image of God" and sketched three stages of the human soul: the ecosystemic stage, as the ultimate source of the soul; the biogenetic stage, as the ground of religious experience; and the sociocultural stage, which has given man a soul essentially different from that of all previous creatures. At the end, he gave the following image of human nature in relation to God:

Salvation is to perceive the glory of God's kingdom and to glory in participating in its continual building. God's kingdom is the succession of actual or real states of the world, among which are the actually selected or ordained ecological niches of life. Man's nature could be likened to an infinite, inverse riverbed in time, a niche in nature through which course God's ever given dissipative streams of energy, destined by God's nature ever to form more complex structures higher above the previous levels of thermodynamic equilibrium (Burhoe 1971c, 202).

God. In another context, Burhoe in fact drew up a list of attributes for God:

Among the main features of traditional attributes or characteristics of *God* as the ultimate reality that determines human destiny are:

1. *God* is the one and only ultimate reality surrounding and infusing man, which created man, and upon which man is utterly dependent.

2. *God* has revealed in part *God's* requirements of and *God's* disposition to men; hence, *God* is not wholly hidden, alien, or mysterious.

3. Yet *God* is in large part hidden, transcendent, beyond what man can fully understand—"supernatural"; hence, the ultimate mystery of *God*.

4. *God* is lawgiver, the reality or power that determines what is right and wrong, and has incarnated or revealed in large measure (by a grace sufficient for the day) the requirements for good and what is to be avoided as evil in the hearts and traditions of creatures.

5. But *God's* continuing program of creation of ever-new stages calls upon most evolving creatures to seek new as well as abide by the established requirements that are still valid—or else disappear from the scene.

6. The guarantee or justification for the hope of the ultimate triumph of *God's* purposes and of all creatures who participate in them, even though any present situation may seem to be disastrously short of this triumph, is revealed by a careful reading of *God's* mighty acts in the past 6×10^3 years.

7. *God* is gracious to man; that is, without any merit on man's part, man has been raised up from the dust and perennially sustained and redeemed from his errancy and given the opportunity to be a conscious cocreator of *God's* evolving Kingdom of Life, as long as man seeks, finds, and executes *God's* requirements (Burhoe 1973c, 422).

In addition, Burhoe says:

In "Natural Selection and God," I have tried to make clear that the scientific pictures show man to be as much a product or creature of a transcendent determiner of destiny as ever the religions hypothesized (Burhoe 1973c, 420).

Enculturation and Freedom. Another schematic presentation is given in "The Civilization of the Future: Ideals and Possibility" (Burhoe 1973b), where he discusses the ideas that civilization is a remarkable system or ecological niche for rapid learning of better ways to live and that the organizing center of a civilization is the human brain. In the human brain are synthesized biological information from the genotype and cultural information from the culturetype. The essential component which gives civilization its character as a system of life is the common culturetype, programmed into each brain in the population. Religion is the agency for enculturating the primary values of the culturetype, without which a culture would cease to be viable.

In an insightful essay occasioned by an IRAS conference on the "Humanizing and Dehumanizing of Man," Burhoe joined with Alfred Emerson to explore the "Evolutionary Aspects of Freedom, Death, and Dignity." Beginning with the definition of freedom as "the liberty to vary that allows choices among alternatives," they explored examples of biological variations and cultural analogues. Because nature imposes restrictions on such freedom to vary, living systems evolve toward the capacity to make choices that are partially preadapted to the conditions which nature imposes. In the human brain, where patterns of choosing are guided by genetic and cultural information, there has evolved the largest capacity of freedom to make viable choices. In their concluding summary they said:

> Man is dependent on the cumulative adaptations of plant, animal, and cultural evolution for the genetic and cultural information that has brought him up from the primitive plants, animals, and societies to his emergence toward increasing social cooperation and high civilization. Contemporary humanity has risen from earlier cultures by means of qualitative and quantitative advancement of emotional and intellectual brain capacities resulting in ever increasing symbolic communication among integrated subcultures. . . . Scientific information seems to reinforce certain elements of religious tradition and may help to provide enlightenment for a more rapid advance in religion's further evolution. Science itself could not survive in a society in which viable motivations for living were not enculturated. It behooves the sciences to take a hint from the evolution of the brain of man not only to provide abstract or incidental information but also to serve humanity's ultimate concerns (Burhoe and Emerson 1974, 179).

A Progress Report: "The Lord of History." In 1975 he published "The Human Prospect and the 'Lord of History' " (Burhoe 1975c). That long essay and its sequel, "What Does Determine Human Destiny?—Science Applied to Interpret Religion" (Burhoe 1977),—which is a response to critics, represent a drawing together of his scattered writings and lectures into a kind of progress report on his proposal for a scientific theology. Responding to the challenges of Robert Heilbroner's *Inquiry into the Human Prospect,* Burhoe elaborated "a scientific picture of religion that will be convincing to the scientific and skeptical minds who have not been provided with much scientific evidence for its virtues and potential" (Burhoe 1975c, 304). He gave an evolutionary interpretation of religion from its ancient biological roots to the emergence of a scientific theology:

> The primary point of this paper is to show that now there seem to be dawning in the recent pictures of man and his relation to the "ultimate reality" as portrayed by the sciences a clarification and substantiation of the basic insights of the great religions, but with much more concrete detail and evidence. It is this synthesis to which I give the name "scientific theology" (Burhoe 1975c, 349).

Central to his interpretation was the thesis that religion is the agent in cultural evolution that has transformed the basic perspectives and motivations of a genus of apes into social and spiritual humans capable of high civilization. The substantiation of the thesis depends upon the hypothesis that there is a selective process operating on sociocultural systems, analogous to biogenetic selection, which can explain the evolution of humans as a symbiosis of genetic and cultural information.

That thesis was further developed in two papers responding to and building upon Donald T. Campbell's controversial presidential address to the American Psychological Association, "On the Conflicts between Biological and Social Evolution and between Psychology and Moral Tradition." Its opening sentence was:

A major thesis of this address is that present-day psychology and psychiatry in all their major forms are more hostile to the inhibitory messages of traditional religious moralizing than is scientifically justified (Campbell 1975, 1103).

In "The Source of Civilization in the Natural Selection of Coadapted Information in Genes and Cultures," Burhoe sought to extend Campbell's interpretation of the function of religion to provide a socially cooperative behavior that genes alone cannot accomplish:

Not only shall I assert the functional utility of religion for social cooperation, I shall move toward demonstrating that the conceptual schemes or myths of religion—about superhuman gods who punish the doers of certain evils and reward the good—that have been selected in cultural evolution are perhaps truer, not only more necessary for societal functioning but also more valid as "ontological" hypotheses, than most modern intellectuals have supposed (Burhoe 1976a, 265).

This paper is of special significance for its elaboration of the concept of coadaptation for understanding the joint operation of selective processes in the physical environment, the genotype, and the culture-type. "The human brain is the integrating mechanism within which three levels of nature are coadapted to produce human nature" (Burhoe 1976a, 281).

For a symposium on sociobiology and religion in 1978, Burhoe defended the thesis that religion is the key and hitherto missing link in the scientific explanation of how ape-men are transformed into civilized altruism. The motivation for defending the thesis was expressed in his opening paragraph: "I am concerned with the development of a more adequate scientific theory of religion, which perchance might revitalize religious belief, reverse a decline in altruism, and prevent a new 'Dark Ages.' " And in the conclusion he said,

I shall conclude by calling attention to the fact that it also follows from this hypothesis concerning the origin of human civilization that religions or some functionally equivalent cultural agencies are essential for any civilization at any stage, including ours, since, beginning with their genetically based rituals and on through myths and theologies, they are the cultural source of coadapted basic values which motivate that genetically selfish ape-man to serve his symbiotic sociocultural organism (Burhoe 1979b, 157).

Thus not only was a scientific theory of religion's role in human evolution necessary to explain the emergence of altruistic cooperation, needed to account for the evolution of civilization (what E. O. Wilson called the "culminating mystery of all biology" [Wilson 1975, 362]), but also it implied that religion, in some form, was essential for the viability of civilization in the future. Thus for our age, threatened with the loss of our religious heritage because of its incredibility in the scientific mind, we need a scientific theology which can revitalize the ancient wisdom about the ultimate destiny and purpose of human life.

THE TEMPLETON PRIZE FOR PROGRESS IN RELIGION

Through his work with the Academy, IRAS, Meadville, CASIRAS, and *Zygon,* Burhoe developed a network (an "invisible college") of a large number of highly respected specialists and scholars in a wide range of disciplines. He devoted great energy both to intellectually relating the contributions of these specialists to his vision for a scientific theology and to providing the organizational structures and opportunities to facilitate communication among these specialists in a congenial atmosphere that was nevertheless conducive to serious intellectual engagement concerning the relation of religion and science. In recognition of his efforts, Burhoe was awarded the prestigious Templeton Prize for Progress in Religion in 1980

for his contributions to the contemporary dialogue between science and religion. During a period when conversation between religion and science was unfashionable, Ralph Burhoe, in his writings, his organizational and promotional skills, and his great personal rapport with both scientists and theologians, has been at the center of a growing discussion, international in scope, and of momentous importance. No other person in the last two decades has had the cumulative impact on this dialogue between professional religionists and scientists as has Ralph Burhoe. His contribution to progress in religion is found in the fact that he, more than any other person now living, has helped to turn modern societies from the growing separation between science and religion and has helped some of our top scientists and theologians move into conversation once again. In addition, he has made theoretical contributions, now receiving international attention, of the highest order towards translating religious truths into scientific concepts. He has worked to show, on broad scientific grounds, the relevance of religion to man's adaptive and moral struggles (Browning 1980).

The Templeton Prize was established in 1972 by John M. Templeton, an American financier, investment adviser, and active Presbyterian layman, because, as he expressed it, "we are trying to say to the world that progress in religion is even more important than progress in anything else—or even all things combined." The prize, the world's largest monetary award, is given in England each year under the patronage of Prince Philip. As the foundation described it,

The objective of the Templeton Foundation Prize is to stimulate the knowledge and love of God on the part of mankind everywhere. . . .
Progress is needed in religion as in all other dimensions of human experience and endeavor. There has been a long departure, at least in Western culture, from the last synthesis when religious knowledge and scientific knowledge were organically related. It is imperative that progress in religion be accelerated as progress in other disciplines takes place. A wider universe demands a deeper awareness of the dimension of the spirit and of its spiritual resources available for man, of the immensity of God, and the divine knowledge and understanding still to be claimed.
The Templeton Foundation Prize serves to stimulate this quest for deeper understanding and pioneering breakthrough in religious knowledge by calling attention annually to the achievements that are being made in this area. It is hoped that there will result from this enterprise a deeper spiritual awareness on the part of men, a better understanding of the meaning of life, a heightened quality of devotion and love, and a greater emphasis on the kind of dedication that brings the human life more into concert with the divine will, thus releasing new and creative energies into human society today (Templeton Foundation 1980).

The first award winner, in 1973, was Mother Teresa of Calcutta. Other winners have been Brother Roger of Taize (1974); Dr. Sarvepalli Radhakrishnan, former president of India (1975); Cardinal Suenens, archbishop of Malines-Brussels (1976); Miss Chiara Lubich (1977); Mr. Nikkyo Niwano (1979); and Billy Graham (1986).

There has been some controversy regarding the establishment of the prize and the process for awarding it. Some were of the opinion that Templeton could have promoted progress in religion in other and better ways than by establishing an annual prize. However, it is well known that science-and-religion is one of Templeton's primary areas of interest, as attested by such typical recipients of the prize as Thomas F. Torrance (1978), Burhoe (1980), Alister C. Hardy (1985), Stanley L. Jaki (1987), and Charles Birch (1990). Templeton was also supportive of the project to establish the Center of Theological Inquiry in Princeton, New Jersey (under James I. McCord), to find common bases for science and religion by bringing scholars from various academic disciplines together for exploration and discussion (Briggs 1984).

In his 1981 book, *The Humble Approach: Scientists Discover God,* Templeton wrote,

> Every person's concept of God is too small. Through humility we can begin to get into true perspective the infinity of God. This is the humble approach. . . .
>
> This book explores the possibility that humility in man's understanding of God may be more fruitful than formal systems of thought which we have inherited, whether they be theistic, pantheistic, or panentheistic. Gradually we may learn to love every one of God's children and be grateful for an increasingly rich diversity of thought emanating from research and worship in every land. One of the purposes of this book is to examine and foster the idea that through a humble approach in knowledge in which we are open-minded and willing to experiment, theology may produce positive results even more amazing than the discoveries of scientists which have electrified the world in this last century. . . .
>
> By reading and writing in this [important and developing] theological field [of science and religion], scientists and other laymen may not only enhance their own spiritual growth but also stimulate progress and expand the whole field of theology in ways that may benefit all. Let us hope that already a spiritual and religious renaissance may have started, and that a great new day may be dawning (Templeton 1981, 3–5).

Templeton also refers to Burhoe's work as "an even more exciting vision of a new theology now being born called the Theology of Science." Templeton attended a Star Island conference and was evidently impressed by the kind of inquiry being stimulated by IRAS. Burhoe was selected by the Templeton Foundation to be nominated for the prize, and in the spring of 1979 Don Browning, of the University of Chicago Divinity School and an associate editor of *Zygon,* was asked to write a nominating letter.

Although some have said that the prize was somewhat discredited because it was awarded to Burhoe, others maintain that such criticism is based solely on ideological differences with the positivistic, naturalistic, and evolutionary philosophy undergirding Burhoe's program. Indeed, such criticisms are similar to those negative reactions to Burhoe's philosophical and methodological commitments which inhibited the program at Meadville and threatened the flourishing of *Zygon,* when adverse forces at the University of Chicago expressed dissatisfaction with Burhoe's editorial policy, which led to the decision of the Press to terminate its agreement to print and distribute the journal. It is also possible that similar ideological differences with Burhoe's vision for revitalizing morality and its religious base in the light of scientific knowledge were at the root of the rejection of the numerous proposals for funding a center for advanced study, in spite of the eminent scholars and scientists who gave their support to them. Burhoe wrote of the relationship between those proposals and the Templeton Prize as follows:

> While CASIRAS vigorously sought funds to finance a sizable and nationally or internationally active center, it seems that most foundations and other institutions that might support CASIRAS have remained up to the present largely incredulous that the sciences could enhance the interpretation and effectiveness of religion or morality. A notable exception was the unsolicited 1980 award of the more than $200,000 Templeton Foundation prize for progress in religion to Burhoe, essentially for the work he had accomplished through *Zygon*, IRAS, and CASIRAS. But most secular foundations and academic institutions seem to feel that religion is only an archaic vestige that must be ignored and will be replaced by a secular ideology, while the religious funds and institutions largely have felt that the sciences are either irrelevant or a dangerous threat to religion, but seldom a resource (Burhoe 1987a, 8).

The Templeton Prize bestowed the long-overdue accolades and well-deserved recognition for Burhoe's work in stimulating the renewal of dialogue between scientists and theologians, as well as his theoretical contributions which helped give shape and coherence to the growing conversation. Indeed, Templeton honored Burhoe with the attributes of visionary and missionary:

> Dr. Burhoe is not only a scientist and a theologian; he is also a visionary and a missionary. He is a missionary for a new reformation, a reformation which may be far more profound and revolutionary than the reformation led by Martin Luther. The vision of Dr. Burhoe is the evolving ancient scriptures (Templeton 1980).

And Lynden Pindling, prime minister of the Bahamas, introduced him by saying,

> Dr. Burhoe, your presence here today as the recipient of the 1980 Award of the Templeton Foundation Prize for Progress in Religion is an indication that the judges of the award, who themselves come from the major religions of the world, feel that you have succeeded, that you are a pioneer, a living example of the resourcefulness of the human mind to continue the quest. Clearly you have demonstrated that the task of creating an acceptable scientific theology has only begun. A beginning which, I am confident, will lead you and your successors to establish a basis that will bolster the faith of many, will enable mankind to be revitalised in the faith and will lead to a better understanding between the peoples of the world (Pindling 1980).

WORK AFTER 1980

After 1980, Burhoe continued to elaborate and refine his position, most notably in five recent essays. The first paper, "Pleasure and Reason as Adaptations to Nature's Requirements," written for a symposium on "Private Interests, Public Good, and the Future of the Environment" in 1981, argues that there is a need in twentieth-century politics and technology for the revitalization of sound religion to provide the noncoerced, cooperative social behavior necessary for the continued health of the commonweal (Burhoe 1982a).

The second paper, written for the Unitarian Universalist *Advance*, "True Spirituality in the Light of the Sciences," is one of the few discussions of the nature of spirituality and religious education in Burhoe's works. True spirituality is built on the coadaptation of our genetic heritage, which structures the instinctual rituals, emotions, and feelings in the lower or inner-brain responses, and our religious-cultural heritage, structured by religious education in the outer cortex. To meet the spiritual needs of a scientific technological environment is the next challenging step in human cultural evolution, and this will require "a reformation of understanding or doctrine, and its propagation, to make possible a union of the spiritual functions and wisdom of the past with the cognitive knowledge of the present" (Burhoe 1981, 16).

An address for the First Unitarian Church of Pittsburgh, Burhoe's third recent essay, is a good outline of his basic theory about the importance of religion in human evolution. It

sketches some elements of a fairly widely substantiated picture compounded from various sciences on how religion became a central, forever necessary element of human nature by its role in the coadaptation that forms a mutually beneficial symbiosis between the hominids and the new transgenetic kingdom of life that emerged in hominid brains as shaped by cultural information (Burhoe 1984b, 11).

In his fourth paper, a chapter for *Cry of the Environment,* a book of religious and ethical resources for rebuilding the Christian creation tradition to deal with the mounting problems of environmental abuse, Burhoe wrote one of his clearest presentations of his position: "a new synthesis of the concepts underlying *evolutionary creation* with *traditional concepts of God.*" There he argued the thesis "that the present environmental crisis, like many other human crises, stems primarily from the failure to communicate our religious tradition's concept of our creator credibly to a scientific-technological world" (Burhoe 1984b, 218).

The last and most recent published paper of significant note is his "War, Peace, and Religion's Biocultural Evolution," which carefully presents the essence of Burhoe's theory of religion in relation to world peace:

If my thesis is correct, that religion is the universal source for internal harmony and cooperation within a society, then one should recognize that all the world's religious cultures, at the underlying level of their basic values, can be interpreted properly today only as a single, universal set of values, common for humanity, even though quite differently expressed in various times and places. This is exactly what is required for the coming one-world village to exist in peace (Burhoe 1987b, 462–63).

It needs to be emphasized that the "problem" of world peace was a fundamental motivation for scientists and scholars at the American Academy of Arts and Sciences who were concerned about science and human values in those formative years when Burhoe was executive officer for the Academy. World peace was also a central concern for the religious leaders of the conferences on the Coming Great Church. It was the coming together of persons in both of these groups that led to the formation of IRAS, which was heir to their concerns and became the center of the tradition which has been traced through Meadville, CASTS, CASIRAS, and *Zygon*. In a real sense, this 1987 article embodies the spirit and wisdom of the forty-year tradition (from 1947 to 1987) which supported, sustained, and tested Burhoe's attempt to formulate his vision for a scientific interpretation of religion as a way of human salvation in the twentieth century.

CONCLUSION

Burhoe's vision for a creative and new theological paradigm in a research and teaching center (Meadville/Lombard) as part of a New Design for theological education did not have the anticipated results. Nonetheless, significant progress was made. IRAS expanded into a membership organization and had broadened its connections by affiliations with the American Association for the Advancement of Science and the Council for the Study of Religion, and had a new generation of leaders. In *Zygon,* the publications program became established as a recognized vehicle for communication among an international community of persons interested in the interpretation of religion in the light of the sciences. The editorial torch had been passed from its founder, and the journal seemed to have a firm foundation of institutional support with its connection to Rollins College. A small volunteer research group, an "invisible college," was functioning in CASIRAS, with its connection to the Lutheran School of Theology and the Cluster of Chicago Theological Schools.

Burhoe's commitment to elaborate and defend his unification of scientific knowledge and traditional religious wisdom through an interpretation of religion in the light of the sciences met resistance largely from those professionally concerned with religious tradition and scholarship. This resistance thwarted his efforts to establish an institutional base. Burhoe was not amenable to compromise and did not encourage a variety of approaches, which a number of persons have seen as a praiseworthy integrity in his commitment and have suggested that his efforts to guide research and discussion along *his* approach prevented the enterprise from becoming too broadly defined and diffuse. In addition, his theoretical work engaged the most prominent issues in the sciences, notably on the relation of biological and cultural evolution, and thus captured the attention and imagination of scientists and a few theologians. Grand in scope, his theory of biocultural evolution is one of very few proposals which can engage theologians, scientists, and philosophers in a discussion of crucial issues concerning religion and values.[3]

EDITOR'S AFTERWORD

Although increasingly hampered by poor health and restricted to his local environs, Ralph Burhoe continued to be active through 1990 in reading, writing, attending Chicago-area meetings, and consulting with individuals and groups. IRAS and *Zygon* continued to thrive; the journal's editorial offices moved to Chicago and the editorial team was substantially augmented with the addition of Philip Hefner as editor in chief and Carol Rausch Gorski as executive editor. Assistant editor Diane Goodman moved from Florida to assume additional responsibilities in the editing process. Burhoe and CASIRAS joined with the Lutheran School of Theology at Chicago (LSTC) to establish the Chicago Center for Religion and Science (CCRS) in January 1988, under the leadership of theologian Philip Hefner and physicist Thomas Gilbert. CCRS houses the *Zygon* editorial office and has continued among its activities to host the annual Chicago Advanced Seminar in Religion and Science that Burhoe began in 1966 at Meadville. CASIRAS was reorganized in December 1989 in order to enhance its effectiveness in the religion-and-science field. Solomon Katz succeeded Donald Harrington as its president, and its membership was substantially increased.

NOTES

1. In a memo to me in March 1987, Burhoe wrote, "If I had not the support for my ideas insofar as they touched the concepts of their own theoretical systems as very credible by some of the greatest intellects of their fields, I never would have had the courage to develop my youthful vision that religious and scientific belief could be unified. My view is a radically new paradigm. Like many past developers of radically new paradigms, I may have to die generally unknown and unaccepted before there are sufficient testings to make recognition possible. But I am still testing and stand ready to test my views against the most recent developments in the various sciences and studies of human nature, religion, and science. My "War, Peace, and Religion's Biocultural Evolution" . . . was sent out in manuscript to several of the people whose judgments and corrections I felt were necessary before publication. These included people near the tops of their fields

. . . such as Don Campbell, Paul McLean, Ladd Prosser, George Pugh, and Roger Sperry. I and the paper were greatly helped by their careful reading, their substantial responses, and their general encouragement.''

2. For example, see Burhoe 1974, Burhoe 1975a, and the March 1977 issue of *Zygon: Journal of Religion and Science* on Burhoe 1975c, to which he responded with Burhoe 1977.

3. The gist of this comment has been attributed to James M. Gustafson in a number of informal conversations. Cf. his ''Theology Confronts Technology and the Life Sciences,'' *Commonweal*, (1978): 391, and his *Ethics from a Theocentric Perspective*, vol. 1, *Theology and Ethics* (Chicago: Univ. of Chicago Press, 1981), p. 258.

REFERENCES

Briggs, Kenneth A. 1984. ''New Center Dedicated to Theology Research.'' *New York Times*, October 10.

Bronowski, J. 1970. ''New Concepts in the Evolution of Complexity: Stratified Stability and Unbounded Plans.'' *Zygon: Journal of Religion and Science* 5 (March): 18–35.

Browning, Don. 1980. Letter of nomination of Burhoe for the Templeton Prize. In the foreword to *The Addresses at the Eighth Presentation of the Templeton Foundation Prize for Progress in Religion*. Dublin, Ireland: Livermore Press.

Burhoe, Ralph Wendell. 1964. ''Contributions to Theology from the Sciences.'' A Prospectus to Meadville Theological School. Mimeo.

―――. 1965. ''A One-Year Trial Balloon towards a Center for Advanced Studies in Theology and the Sciences.'' Chicago: Burhoe Archives. Mimeo.

―――. 1966a. Editorial. *Zygon: Journal of Religion and Science* 1 (March): 1–10.

―――. 1966b. ''The Growth of Symbols of Sacred Goals in Terms of a Scientific World View.'' Paper presented for a symposium, The Dialogue of Change: Systems in Interaction, at the annual meeting of the American Association for the Advancement of Science, December 27, at Washington, D.C.

―――. 1967. ''To Friends of Frances (Bickford) Burhoe, 4 October 1909–19 August 1967.'' Chicago: Burhoe Archives. Self-published booklet.

―――. 1968. Editorial. *Zygon: Journal of Religion and Science* 3 (March): 2–5.

―――. 1969. ''Values via Science.'' *Zygon: Journal of Religion and Science* 4 (March): 65–99.

―――. 1970a. Memo on the Center and Other Institutions. Chicago: Burhoe Archives. May 4.

―――. 1970b. Editorial. *Zygon: Journal of Religion and Science* 5 (June): 98–101.

―――. 1970c. ''Commentary on J. Bronowski's New Concepts in the Evolution of Complexity.'' *Zygon: Journal of Religion and Science* 5 (June): 98–101.

―――. 1970d. ''Potentials for Religion from the Sciences.'' *Zygon: Journal of Religion and Science* 5 (June): 110–29.

―――. 1971a. ''Notes on the Meadville/Lombard Center on Science and Human Destiny.'' Paper distributed to the faculty and Long-Range Planning Committee of the Board of Trustees. Chicago: Burhoe Archives. Mimeo.

―――. 1971b. ''What Specifies the Values of the Man-Made Man?'' *Zygon: Journal of Religion and Science* 6 (September): 224–46.

―――, ed. 1971c. *Science and Human Values in the 21st Century*. Philadelphia: Westminster Press.

―――. 1972a. Editorial. *Zygon: Journal of Religion and Science* 7 (March): 2–5.

―――. 1972b. ''Natural Selection and God.'' *Zygon: Journal of Religion and Science* 7 (March): 30–63.

―――. 1972c. ''Evolving Cybernetic Machinery and Human Values.'' *Zygon: Journal of Religion and Science* 7 (September): 188–209.

―――. 1972d. ''Proposal to Establish an Independent Center for Advanced Study in Religion and Science.'' *Zygon: Journal of Religion and Science* 7 (September): 168–83.

―――. 1972e. ''The Control of Behavior: Human and Environmental.'' *Journal of Environmental Health* 35 (November/December): 247–58.

————. 1973a. "The Institute on Religion in an Age of Science—A Twenty-Year View." *Zygon: Journal of Religion and Science* 8 (March): 59–80.

————. 1973b. "The Civilization of the Future: Ideals and Possibility." *Philosophy Forum* 13 (June): 149–77.

————. 1973c. "The Concepts of 'God' and 'Soul' in a Scientific View of Human Purpose." *Zygon: Journal of Religion and Science* 8 (September/December): 412–42.

————. 1973d. "The World System and Human Values." In *The World System: Models, Norms, Applications,* ed. Erwin Laszlo, 161–85. New York: George Braziller.

————. 1974. Editorial. *Zygon: Journal of Religion and Science* 9 (March): 2–6.

————. 1975a. Editorial. *Zygon: Journal of Religion and Science* 10 (March): 2–11.

————. 1975b. "Note on the Institutional and Financial Support of *Zygon.*" *Zygon: Journal of Religion and Science* 10 (March): 113–24.

————. 1975c. "The Human Prospect and the 'Lord of History.' " *Zygon: Journal of Religion and Science* 10 (September): 299–375.

————. 1976a. "The Source of Civilization in the Natural Selection of Coadapted Information in Genes and Culture." *Zygon: Journal of Religion and Science* 11 (September): 263–303.

————. 1976b. "The Nature of Man as a Niche in Nature and as an Image of God." In *Belonging and Alienation: Religious Foundations for the Human Future,* ed. Philip Hefner and W. Widick Schroeder. Chicago: Center for the Scientific Study of Religion.

————. 1977. "What Does Determine Human Destiny?—Science Applied to Interpret Religion." *Zygon: Journal of Religion and Science* 12 (December): 336–89.

————. 1978. Editorial. *Zygon: Journal of Religion and Science* 13 (December): 250–56.

————. 1979a. Editorial. *Zygon: Journal of Religion and Science* 14 (March): 3–5.

————. 1979b. "Religion's Role in Human Evolution: The Missing Link between Ape-Man's Selfish Genes and Civilized Altruism." *Zygon: Journal of Religion and Science* 14 (June): 135–62.

————. 1981. "True Spirituality in the Light of the Sciences." Unitarian Universalist Advance Study Paper no. 17.

————. 1982a. "Pleasure and Reason as Adaptations to Nature's Requirements." *Zygon: Journal of Religion and Science* 17 (June): 113–31.

————. 1982b. "Ralph Wendell Burhoe." In *Harvard Class of 1932, Fiftieth Anniversary Report,* pp. 79–86. Cambridge, Mass.: Harvard University.

————. 1984a. "Religion's Importance as Seen in Natural History." *Religious Humanism* 18 (Summer/Autumn): 110–17, 178–85.

————. 1984b. "Cosmic Evolutionary Creation and Christian God." In *Cry of the Environment: Rebuilding the Christian Creation Tradition,* ed. Philip N. Joranson and Ken Butigan, pp. 218–52. Santa Fe, N.M.: Bear & Co.

————. 1987a. "The Center for Advanced Study in Religion and Science and *Zygon: Journal of Religion and Science*—A Twenty-Year View." *Zygon: Journal of Religion and Science* 22 (Twentieth Anniversary Issue): 5–19.

————. 1987b. "War, Peace, and Religion's Biocultural Evolution." *Zygon: Journal of Religion and Science* 21 (December): 439–72.

————. 1988. Papers by Ralph Wendell Burhoe concerning Religion in the Light of the Sciences. Chicago: Burhoe Archives.

Burhoe, Ralph Wendell, and Alfred E. Emerson. 1974. "Evolutionary Aspects of Freedom, Death, and Dignity." *Zygon: Journal of Religion and Science* 9 (June): 156–82.

Campbell, Donald T. 1975. "On the Conflicts between Biological and Social Evolution and between Psychology and Moral Tradition." *American Psychologist* 30:1103–26. Reprinted in *Zygon: Journal of Religion and Science* 11 (September 1976): 167–208.

Cauthen, Kenneth. 1969. *Science, Secularization & God: Toward a Theology of the Future.* Nashville: Abingdon Press.

Clark, John Ruskin. 1977. *The Great Living System: New Answers from the Sciences to Old Religious Questions.* Pacific Grove, Calif.: Boxwood Press.

Gentner, Donald R. 1968. "The Scientific Basis of Some Concepts of Pierre de Chardin." *Zygon: Journal of Religion and Science* 3 (December): 432–41.
Greeley, Dana McLean. 1971. *25 Beacon Street and Other Recollections*. Boston: Beacon Press.
Meadville Theological School. 1964. *Announcement of the New Design of Theological Education at Meadville Theological School of Lombard College*. Chicago: Meadville Theological School.
Milburn, Patrick. 1971. "Review of *Zygon*." *Main Currents in Modern Thought* 28: 71–72. Reprinted in *Zygon: Journal of Religion and Science* 7 (March): 64–67.
Northrop, F. S. C. 1966. "Commentary on Theological Resources from the Physical Sciences." *Zygon: Journal of Religion and Science* 1 (March): 37.
Peters, Karl. 1987. "The Contours of an Emerging Territory: Impressions of Twenty Years of *Zygon: Journal of Religion and Science*." *Zygon: Journal of Religion and Science* 22 (Twentieth Anniversary Issue): 44.
Pindling, Lyndon O. 1980. "The Address of the Right Honourable Lyndon O. Pindling, Prime Minister of the Commonwealth of the Bahamas." In *The Addresses at the Eighth Presentation of the Templeton Foundation Prize for Progress in Religion*. Dublin, Ireland: Lismore Press.
Riggan, George Arkell. 1968. "Testing the Teilhardian Foundations." *Zygon: Journal of Religion and Science* 3 (September): 259–313.
———. 1987. "The Center for Advanced Study in Religion and Science: A Personal Perspective." *Zygon: Journal of Religion and Science* 22 (Twentieth Anniversary Issue): 31.
Sutherland, Malcolm R., Jr. 1987. "Reflections on the First Twenty Years of CASIRAS: A Personal Review." *Zygon: Journal of Religion and Science* 22 (Twentieth Anniversary Issue): 20–27.
Templeton, John M. 1980. "The Address of Mr. John M. Templeton, Founder of the Templeton Foundation." In *The Addresses at the Eighth Presentation of the Templeton Foundation Prize for Progress in Religion*. Dublin, Ireland: Lismore Press.
———. 1981. *The Humble Approach: Scientists Discover God*. New York: Seabury Press.
Templeton Foundation. 1980. "The Objectives." In *The Addresses at the Eighth Presentation of the Templeton Foundation Prize for Progress in Religion*. Dublin, Ireland: Lismore Press.
Wilson, E. O. 1975. *Sociobiology: The New Synthesis*. Cambridge, Mass.: Harvard Univ. Press. Quoted in Burhoe 1979b.

Index

Burhoe, Frances, 4, 5, 9, 120
Burhoe, Ralph Wendell—Academy
  years, 11-16
  awards, 20, 130-133
  communication, 6, 7, 11
  criticisms of, 60-64, 113, 135-136
  formative years, 1-26, 29
  intellect, 121-130, 136n
  lectures, 44, 77, 81, 89-90, 98-99,
    100, 121, 134
  offices, 11-13, 29, 67-68, 73-74,
    77-104, 109, 114, 117-119,
    121, 130, 135
  religious life, 6, 10, 13, 24, 88
  retirement, 114, 119
  theology, 13-14, 23, 77-104,
    112-113, 116, 121-129
  Zygon publication, 109-113, 121,
    132

Cabot, Richard, 6
Campbell, Donald T., 103, 129,
  137n
Cannon, W. B., 3
Carnap, Rudolf, 17, 18
Carnegie Corporation grant, 15
Carnes, Paul, 53
CASIRAS. *See* Center for
  Advanced Study in Religion and
  Science
CASTS. *See* Center for Advanced
  Study in Theology and the
  Sciences
Causality, 96, 97
Cauthen, Kenneth, 117, 118
Center for Advanced Study in
  Theology and the Sciences, 109,
  112, 115-119, 122, 135
Center for Advanced Theological
  Studies, 69
Center for Integration of Religion
  and Science, 70-72
Center of Theological Inquiry,
  Princeton, N.J., 131
Chaisson, Eric, 104n
Chautauqua Institution, 44

Chicago Advanced Seminar in
  Religion and Science, 136
Chicago Center for Religion and
  Science, 136
Chicago Cluster of Theological
  Schools, 114, 118, 119, 135
Christian theistic humanism, 23
Civilization, 36, 81, 82, 104. *See
  also* Culturetype
Clark, John Ruskin, 117
Clark, Walter H., 19, 43
Clergy—scientific interests, 22,
  24, 35, 68
Colgate-Rochester Divinity School,
  44
Collingwood, R. G., 84
"Colloquium on Man", 117
"Coming Great Church"
  conferences, 22-25, 39, 52, 135
Committee for the Social Scientific
  Study of Religion, 19
Committee on Science and Values,
  16, 21-22, 24-25, 35, 51, 77
Community Church, Boston, 5
Conference on Religion in an
  Age of Science, 25-26
Consciousness, 97
Cooperation, social, 129
Copernican revolution, 92
Cosmic evolution. *See* Evolution
Cosmic law, 58-62, 99, 100
Cosmic reality, 84, 87, 90, 95,
  100, 103
Cosmology, 31-32, 56-58, 60, 84, 92
Cosmotype, 20, 100
Council for the Study of Religion,
  135
Covenant relationship, 57-58
Crane School of Religion, 44, 75n
Creation, 47, 84, 98. *See also*
  God—Creator
Cultural evolution, 15-16, 58, 65,
  99-104, 110, 125, 128-129
Culture and religion, 13-14, 32,
  35-36, 46, 56, 59-60, 81-84,
  94, 129
Culture and science, 36, 43, 46

Harvard Divinity School, 75n
Harvard University, 1-4
Hayward, John F., 109, 118
Hefner, Philip, 105n, 114, 136
Heilbroner, Robert, 128
Hoagland, Hudson, 11, 15, 21, 26n, 41
Hocking, W. E., 1
Holton, Gerald, 14
Homeostasis (term), 3
Hooten, E. A., 2
Hoskins, Roy G., 21-22
Human condition, 9-10, 45-48, 83-84
Human destiny, 85, 118-119, 123, 125, 128
Human life. *See* Life; Self
Human nature, 25, 39, 83-84, 103, 122, 126
Human predicament, 4-5, 83-84, 96
Human survival. *See* Salvation
Human values. *See* Values
Human welfare, 13, 25, 33, 35, 80
Humanism, 23
Huxley, Julian, 70

Idenes (term), 63
Illingworth, Robert, 22
Image of God, 126
Immortality, 47, 100-102
Institute for the Unity of Science, 16-19, 22
Institute on Man and Science, Rensselaerville, N.Y., 119
Interiorization of religion, 80, 83
International Encyclopedia of Unified Science, 17
Institute on Religion in an Age of Science
    Advisory Board, 26, 30-33, 40-44
    Burhoe's assessment of, 42-43, 116
    Committee on Science and Human Values, 119
    Conferences. *See* Star Island
    development, 16, 22, 25,

29-49, 51-52, 67
goals, 25, 31-35, 42-43, 51, 135
Mission to theological schools, 43-44, 70
Proposal for Development of Program, 35-37, 51
publication program, 33, 37, 43, 109, 119
IRAS. *See* Institute on Religion in an Age of Science

Jaki, Stanley L., 131
Jesus of history, 23
Joergensen, Joergen, 17, 18
Jones, Howard Mumford, 12, 13
Journal for the Scientific Study of Religion, 19
Judeo-Christian heritage, 79, 80, 81, 97, 111, 112

Kallen, Horace, 19
Kant, Immanuel, 99
Katz, Solomon, 114, 136
Kemble, Edwin C., 2, 41, 42, 43
Kennedy, John F., 14
Killian, James R., 44
Kingdom of God, 126-127
Kluckhohn, Clyde, 81
Knowledge
    evolution, 36-38, 58-59, 65, 62-63, 95-96, 123
    humanization, 12-13
    integration, 17-18, 21, 24-25, 63, 86. *See also* Science and knowledge
Kosmos, 57

Lakatos, Imre, 104n
Language, 15, 17-18, 58, 60, 63, 96. *See also* Universal scientific language
Lash, Nicholas, 84
Law of God, 57
Liberal education, 81
Liberal religion, 51-55, 60, 62, 64-68

Pius XII, Pope, 24
Positivism, 17, 24, 78, 87, 90,
  92-95. *See also* Logical positivism
Prosser, Ladd, 137n
Psalms—poetic metaphysics, 98
Pugh, George, 137n

Radhakrishnan, Sarvepalli, 131
Rational/mystical dichotomy, 1
Reality, 25, 36, 40, 43, 96
Religion
  credibility, 80, 83
  definition, 32, 122
  evolution, 16, 38-40, 59,
    62-63, 65-66, 83, 85, 122,
    125-126. *See also* Evolution—
    Religious factor.
  function, 5, 7, 40-42, 85-89
  revitalization, 16, 52-54,
    80-85,
    94, 109, 111, 115, 125
Religion and culture. *See* Culture
  and religion
Religion and science, 14, 34-36,
  39, 43, 60-68, 90-94
  integration, 23-25, 34-36, 39,
    45-48, 63-64, 66-68, 70-71,
    86, 90-94, 135, 136n
  method, 13, 15-25, 37, 41-42,
    48, 54-55, 63-64, 66, 79, 111
Religion and Science and the
  Frontiers of Learning, 74n
Religions, 23, 39. 85. *See also* Beliefs
Religious truth. *See* Truth
Revelation, 47, 65-66, 78-79
Ricoeur, Paul, 112
Riggan, George, 117, 118, 119
Rockefeller Foundation Grant, 18
Roger of Taize, 131
Rollins College—*Zygon* offices,
  114, 135
Rotch, Abbott Lawrence, 8
Rutledge, Lyman V., 22, 25, 41, 42

Saint Lawrence University,
  Theological School, 44

Salvation, 25, 29, 32, 33, 35, 36,
  38-39, 45-48, 70, 77, 85, 86,
  90-91, 94, 102, 104, 110, 111,
  126
"Salvation in the twentieth
  century", 77
Saunders, Frederick A., 2
Schlick, Moritz, 17
Scholars—Burhoe's relation with,
  115-118, 130
Schroeder, W. Widick, 105n
Schrödinger, Erwin, 98
Science—philosophy. *See Philosophy
  of science*
Science and knowledge, 20, 45-49,
  63, 88, 125, 135-136
Science and religion. *See* Religion
  and science
Science and technology, 15, 21, 82
Scientific method, 13, 16, 37, 93,
  123
Scientific religion, 45-48, 63, 111
Scientific theology, 18, 29, 36-39,
  45-48, 77-84, 116, 121-122,
  125, 128
Secularism, 13-14, 81, 82
Self, 83-84
Sewell, Elizabeth, 112
Shapley, Harlow, 11, 21, 26n, 30,
  31, 43, 45, 98, 105n
Skinner, B. F., 42, 97, 99, 102
Skinner, Clarence, 5
Social behavior, 103, 129
Social sciences, 20, 112
Society for the Scientific Study
  of Religion, 16, 19-21
Sociobiology, 129-130
Sociocultural evolution, 15,
  102-104, 126, 129, 130
Sociology of religion, 20
Sorokin, Pitirim, 19
Soul, 20, 47-48, 100-104, 126
Soul and spirit, 61
Sperry, Roger, 137n
Spiritual crisis, 82, 84, 134
Spirituality, 134
SSSR. *See* Society for the Scientific
  Study of Religion